INTRODU

Welcome to *Create.Repeat.*

If you picked up this book, chances are you're a creative person. Or you're drawn to creative people. Or maybe you're just trying to figure out what the hell 'being creative' even means. Whatever pulled you here, it matters. You're here, and that means something.

Creativity isn't linear. It's a cycle. A rhythm. A rising and a falling. You'll have breakthroughs and breakdowns. Momentum and melt-downs. Days when ideas pour out of you like water and days when showing up feels impossible. This book was built for all of it. For every version of you that chooses to stay in the game.

Opening these pages is an act of homecoming – a recognition of that deep knowing within your soul. The stirring. The creative force that has been quietly waiting for permission to take up space again. Here it is. Here you are.

For us, that moment came out of desperation. After three years of burnout disguised as busyness, we hit the kind of low that made us question everything we thought we knew about being creative. We were living through a pandemic, navigating job instability, wrestling with depression, and carrying a lot of doubt we couldn't quite shake.

We can't point to a single, dramatic moment when everything fell apart. It was more like a slow fade – the dimming of a candle. Little by little, the light thinned, until one day, it was simply gone. Something inside us had gone quiet.

We were still creating, technically. We were producing, publishing and putting things out into the world. But not from the heart. Not from that sacred, soul-deep place.

We weren't making art, we were making content. And there's a difference. Content performs. Art expresses. Content chases approval. Art tells the truth. What we were missing was expression – the raw, honest kind. We had to remember why we ever wanted to make anything at all.

So, we gave ourselves a challenge. Thirty days. No goals, no gold stars. Just a promise: create something – *anything* – every single day. No perfection. No pressure. Just the rhythm. Create. Then repeat.

A new Instagram account became a thread we clung to. A simple rhythm at first – personal, quiet. But over time, it began to mend us. And then something even bigger happened: other artists and creatives found their way to us. They needed it too. This book is the living proof of that rhythm.

WHAT YOU'RE HOLDING

Inside these pages are 365 micro-chapters – ideas, reflections, practices and prompts. Each one is designed to reconnect you with your creativity – not the polished, filtered kind, but the messy, emotional, soul-level kind that makes you feel alive in your body again.

Start on 1 January. Or 5 April. Or a random Tuesday when you finally feel ready. The date doesn't matter. What matters is that you begin. You can read one a day or ten in one sitting. You can skip around, flip to whatever calls you, and come back whenever you need a push. Write in the margins. Highlight it. Bend pages. Leave coffee stains. Make it yours.

Create.Repeat

Zack Evans is a writer, creative director, and self-described recovering content creator who's on a mission to help artists reconnect with their work and with themselves. He came up during the wild heyday of *BuzzFeed*, producing hundreds of viral videos that reached millions, and is now co-founder of Create.Repeat: part newsletter, part podcast and part creative studio.

Morgan Evans is a writer, content producer, co-founder of Create. Repeat and the founder of Season of Sunday, a mental health clothing brand featured on *The Today Show* and embraced by artists, creators and celebrities alike. She's also the voice behind the Substack *Is Anyone Else Spiraling?*, where she writes personal essays about mental health, female friendship, creativity and the hard work of learning to move through the spiral.

They live in Los Angeles.

Create.Repeat

365 DAYS OF CREATIVITY

ZACK AND MORGAN EVANS

MICHAEL  JOSEPH

PENGUIN MICHAEL JOSEPH

UK | USA | Canada | Ireland | Australia
India | New Zealand | South Africa

Penguin Michael Joseph is part of the Penguin Random House group of companies
whose addresses can be found at global.penguinrandomhouse.com

Penguin Random House UK,
One Embassy Gardens, 8 Viaduct Gardens, London SW11 7BW

penguin.co.uk

First published 2025

001

Set in 12.2/15 pt Garamond Premier Pro
Typeset by Six Red Marbles UK, Thetford, Norfolk
Printed and bound in Great Britain by Clays Ltd, Elcograf S.p.A.

The authorized representative in the EEA is Penguin Random House Ireland,
Morrison Chambers, 32 Nassau Street, Dublin D02 YH68

A CIP catalogue record for this book is available from the British Library

ISBN: 978-0-241-73778-1

Penguin Random House is committed to a sustainable future
for our business, our readers and our planet. This book is made from
Forest Stewardship Council® certified paper

To Amanda and Steve.
Thank you for betting on us, believing in us
and building with us.
Create.Repeat exists because of you.

Some entries will meet you in your mess. Others will push you to move. All of them are invitations. This book isn't about waiting for inspiration – we've learned, again and again, we cannot rely on that. This is about discipline, not motivation. Writing when you're tired. Making something when you're unsure. Showing up even when your inner critic is screaming.

Somewhere around Day 41, or 97, or 213, you might look up and realize something strange has happened. You're starting to feel different. Not because you've become some wildly productive machine, but because you've reconnected with your soul voice – your curiosity, your confidence, your imagination.

That's the shift. That's the homecoming. Fall off track? Stand back up. No shame. No scorecards. No need for gold stars. This isn't about doing it right. It's about showing up for the rhythm that's already inside you.

WHO THIS BOOK IS FOR

This book is for the ones who've said:

'I don't have time.'
'I'm not ready.'
'I'm stuck.'
'I'm not good enough.'
'I missed my chance.'
'I don't know where to start.'
'I don't have anything to say.'
'I'm too tired.'
'I can't focus.'
'I always quit halfway through.'

And it's also for the ones who've whispered:

'I think I have more to give.'
'I have something to express.'
'I want to take up space.'
'I'm ready to begin.'
'I want to feel alive again.'
'I'm willing to try.'
'I'm tired of waiting for permission.'
'I'm ready to bet on myself.'
'I want to see what happens if I don't give up this time.'

If any of that sounds like you, here's what we want you to know:

You are ready.
You are enough.
You do not need permission.
You never have.
But if you've been waiting for it – this is it.

Create.Repeat is for anyone who wants to stop overthinking and start expressing. For the dreamers, the doers, the once-a-year painters, the late-night writers, the burned-out designers, the inspired-and-overwhelmed, the multi-hyphenates and the in-betweeners.

We don't have all the answers, but we do know this: if you create and repeat, something will shift. Something will move. And eventually, something will break open.

So, step up. Create with your whole heart. Create through doubt. Create through joy. Just create. And then repeat. Again and again.

We're here with you, because we are you. Create. Repeat. When you create from your soul and we create from ours, we are no longer separate. We are one.

With deep love,
Zack & Morgan

DAY 1: FIND THE KNOWING

Being an artist is about a deep knowing – not guessing, not over-thinking, just knowing. If you don't believe in it, you're not truly doing it. The beginning of a creative journey is often sparked by what we typically call INSPIRATION. But let's redefine that a bit. Let's call it KNOWING. Knowing goes beyond mere inspiration; it's deep intuition, a profound understanding that comes from within. Getting an idea or that sudden burst of inspiration might seem like it comes from nowhere, but to truly bring it to life, you need more than just inspiration. This knowing, it's like it's already inside you. You don't have to search for it; you just have to trust in it, keep showing up and do the work.

CHALLENGE

- What do you know about yourself? Set a timer for 5 minutes and list as many things as you can. These can be emotional truths, interesting facts or life experiences. Your list can be as profound or as simple as you prefer.
- How can you embed this knowing in your creative routine? Set a timer for 5 more minutes and list as many ideas as you can that derive from what you know about yourself and the world around you. Turn your Knowing into Inspiration.

DAY 2: CREATE FROM THE SOURCE

Create from the deepest part of who you are. The soul of you. If you don't share your truth, no one will. Your influences will come from various sources. By taking the time to recognize and embrace these influences, you can gain valuable insights into your creative process. By understanding why you think the way you do, you gain a deeper awareness of what sets you apart as a creator.

When you fully embrace your voice, you empower yourself to create from a place of truth and authenticity. Your work becomes a reflection of your unique vision and perspective, resonating with genuine sincerity. So, as you step into inspiration, remember to honour and embrace the voice that is uniquely yours.

CHALLENGE

- What works inspired you as a kid and brought you on to the creative path? Write them down and reflect on what it was that excited you about them.
- If there was a single characteristic or value that resonated with you and which you'd like your works to reflect, what would it be? Once you've identified it, treat it as the North Star of your creative process.
- Build a playlist of songs that take you back to simpler days and favourite productions. Whenever you feel disconnected from your creative voice, let this collection remind you of your source.

DAY 3: UNBLOCK YOUR DREAMS

Let's clarify something: don't mistake your feelings of unworthiness for doubts about your artistic abilities. Often, it's not your art that's the problem – it's you. It's crucial to acknowledge this. You have the talent and capability to create and live the best artistic life possible if you feel the pull and motivation towards it. However, if deep down you don't believe you deserve it, you'll continually sabotage your dreams. Let's address this issue head-on and not let it affect our creativity. Remove your ego from the mix and the blocks will disappear, too. All you need to do is start believing. You really have nothing to lose. You can only win.

CHALLENGE

Affirmations can be powerful tools to reshape your mindset and unleash your creative potential. Here are some empowering sayings you can adopt:

- My creativity knows no bounds; I am limitless.
- I am worthy of expressing my unique voice through my art.
- I embrace imperfection as a stepping stone to greatness.
- I release the need for approval and create authentically from my heart.
- Obstacles are opportunities for innovation and growth.
- My art has the power to inspire, uplift and change lives.

DAY 4: MAKE IT HAPPEN

When was the last time you felt that fire in your soul – the kind of hunger that refuses to be ignored? Let today be the day you answer it. Not someday. Not when it's convenient. Today.

Unleash your creativity with fearless abandon. Pour yourself into your craft, in whatever way calls to you. Paint, write, build, design – just create. No overthinking. No waiting for permission. The moment is now.

Let's tap into the energy that turns visions into reality. Show up for your art with unwavering belief. The only thing standing between you and the work you're meant to do is the decision to begin. So, begin.

CHALLENGE

Set a timer for 15–30 minutes and challenge yourself to create something within that time frame. It could be a quick sketch, a short poem, a piece of music or even a mini dance routine. The key is to focus on the process rather than the outcome and allow yourself to experiment without judgement.

DAY 5: TEAR THE LABELS

Give yourself permission to not have all the answers. Read what excites you, not what feels expected. Listen to something unfamiliar. Start a conversation outside your norm. Let yourself explore, stumble and feel foolish – because that's where growth begins.

Don't label yourself. Be free. Labels, like cement, can restrict us to predefined roles and identities. It's like being told you can only be one thing, whether it's a musician, a painter or a digital marketer. But why should we let the pressures of society dictate who we are or what we can become? What if, instead of confining ourselves to labels, we embraced the idea of being master interpreters of the world?

Life isn't about choosing one path – it's about collecting experiences, skills and passions that shape who we are. Embrace the fluidity of your creativity. Be a musician today, a storyteller tomorrow, a strategist next week. Let curiosity, not labels, guide you.

CHALLENGE

Where would your creative process take you if you removed all the labels? Imagine you were not constrained by your job or social media bio and write down five to ten things that interest you and that you would like to explore. Then find a way to incorporate them into your art or content.

DAY 6: THERE IS NO FINISH LINE

The creative journey is not linear; it's a cycle of learning, experimenting, failing and evolving. We must shift our focus. There is no finish line; it's an endless journey. Keep moving forward. We all yearn for the moment when our project is complete, a masterpiece to be admired and checked off our list. But the reality is that the act of creation itself is the true essence of the experience; there will be more days when getting out of bed feels like a monumental task than days when we're releasing our greatest art.

Are you prepared for that? Can you embrace and accept the process for what it is? This is where the true meaning lies – in the space between Creating and Repeating. This is where growth happens, lessons are learned and where our creativity blossoms.

CHALLENGE

What was the last project you started but never completed, and why did you stop? What did you learn from the process? How has it helped you grow, even if the final product was never realized? Commit to a chosen creative act for 15 minutes per day for the next week and watch the progress unravel. No thinking, just creating.

DAY 7: STAY CURIOUS

Look beyond the familiar, question the status quo and imagine what could be. It is in the pursuit of the unseen and the yet-to-be-discovered that life becomes richer, more vibrant and infinitely more interesting.

As creatives, we're inherently called to be empathetic, to understand and connect with the world around us. Let's commit to staying open-minded and curious. Rather than allowing life to passively occur around us, let's actively engage with it, shaping our experiences and growth in the process.

CHALLENGE

Today, talk to someone you don't usually interact with. It could be a stranger, the barista you get your coffee from every day, or perhaps a chat with your grandma about something you've never talked about before. Ask them about their life and listen attentively. Be curious about their viewpoint and later reflect on what insight you've gained from the interaction.

DAY 8: CREATE YOUR PURPOSE

Embrace the freedom to explore the vast landscapes of your imagination and forge a purpose that resonates with the core of who you are. You are not confined to your current circumstances. You possess the power to alter the trajectory of your life. Stop making excuses for why change seems impossible. You have the capacity to craft a purposeful existence that resonates deeply with your soul. If you find yourself perpetually discontented and unfulfilled, recognize that you are the master of your own destiny. You are the brick wall in your own life – the obstacle standing between you and the life you desire. Embrace this realization as an opportunity for reinvention and embark on the journey to redefine yourself.

CHALLENGE

- Reflect on Your Passion: What subjects or themes do you find yourself drawn to? What activities make you lose track of time? Pay attention to these clues as they can point you towards your creative purpose.
- Identify Your Values: What causes or issues are you passionate about? How can you use your creativity to advocate for these causes or make a positive impact in the world?
- Explore Strengths and Skills: What are you naturally good at? What skills have you developed over time? How can you leverage these strengths in your creative endeavours?
- Listen to Your Gut: Trust your instincts and follow your curiosity, even if it leads you down unconventional paths.
- Set Goals and Take Action: Break down your goals into smaller, manageable steps and create a plan for how you will accomplish them.

DAY 9: I AM

What's your 'I AM'? Have you taken the time to consider this? How often do you let your mind wander aimlessly, caught in a cycle of self-doubt and indecision? If you want to be an author, then **write**. If you want to be a painter, then **paint**. Writers write, and painters paint. It's that simple. Step into your identity and embrace it wholeheartedly. Believe in your potential and your passion. You are the driving force behind your journey, and when you commit to your 'I AM', you will become unstoppable. So, what's your 'I AM'? Reflect on it, own it and then take action. The world is waiting for your unique voice, your perspective and your creativity. Don't hold back – become who you were meant to be.

CHALLENGE

Write down your 'I AM' statement – who you are and who you aspire to be. For example, 'I am a writer,' 'I am an artist,' or 'I am a creator.'

DAY 10: PROGRESS, NOT PERFECTION

Creativity isn't about perfection – it's about showing up, again and again, despite the uncertainty. The dreams we chase won't appear overnight, but that doesn't mean they aren't unfolding.

You must fall in love with the process, of embracing the slow build, the missteps and the breakthroughs. Some days will feel like a surge of inspiration, while others may feel like walking through fog. But every moment spent creating – no matter how small – is a step forward.

Progress isn't always loud or obvious. Sometimes, it's in the quiet persistence, in the willingness to keep going even when the finish line feels out of reach. Trust that even when it seems like nothing is happening, your work is growing, evolving, becoming. Keep creating and keep believing. It will work.

CHALLENGE

Make progress today, no matter how big or small. Advance your project by moving the needle forward in any way you can.

DAY 11: GREAT ART COMES FROM GREAT EMPATHY

Don't numb yourself. Don't turn off the parts of you that allow you to feel deeply. Don't be afraid. The beauty of being broken is that you can create from the ashes. Let the ashes fall away so you can awaken. Sadness isn't the only thing you allow yourself to feel. If you constantly shut off your emotions, you'll turn off the good stuff too. Don't block out happiness and joy. You need the waves of emotions to create art that resonates.

Empathy is a practice. It might come easier to some, but as artists, aren't we called to empathy? Empathy is the ability to understand and share the feelings of another person. It involves recognizing and appreciating another's emotional state. Empathy allows us to connect on an emotional level, showing compassion and understanding without necessarily having experienced the same situation ourselves.

Channel that empathy into your art. There is no better mindset for creation. So don't be afraid. Just feel.

CHALLENGE

Spend a few minutes today observing people around you – whether in person or in a photo – and imagine their stories and emotions. Write a brief narrative or description about what they might be feeling and how you relate to those feelings. Use this exercise to practise empathy and consider how these imagined emotions can inspire your creative work.

DAY 12: IT'S SUPPOSED TO BE HARD

It's supposed to be hard. Let's not forget that. We may marvel at the achievements of visionaries like Eadweard Muybridge, who captured the first motion picture of a galloping horse, but behind their revolutionary feats lies a story of relentless determination.

If these monumental tasks were easy, everyone would be doing them. When faced with the challenge, remember to have grace for yourself. Without grace, you put your creativity and motivation at risk. Keep your head down, stay focused and persevere through the onslaught of doubts that may come your way. Push past the obstacles, for it's in overcoming them that you'll truly soar.

CHALLENGE

Give yourself some grace today.

DAY 13: DON'T LIMIT YOURSELF

Why do we insist on placing so many limitations on ourselves? It's like we're determined to suck all the excitement out of our creative project before we've even begun. Is this some form of art self-sabotage? We seem to always be finding reasons to hold ourselves back, creating arbitrary rules and excuses that keep us from diving into our passion projects with full enthusiasm. It's time to break free from this cycle of self-sabotage and embrace the freedom to explore and create without constraints. Stop making excuses and get back to what truly matters – bringing your creative visions to life.

CHALLENGE

Write down any limiting beliefs or assumptions you have about your creative project or goals. These could include statements such as 'I'm not talented enough,' or 'There's only one right way to do this.' Acknowledge these thoughts without judgement, and then challenge them by asking yourself, 'What if this weren't true?'

DAY 14: EMBRACE THE GOOD VIBES

The idea of the tortured artist has been romanticized for too long. While it can be tempting to gather with fellow pessimists and commiserate about feeling stuck in a bleak world, the reality is that dwelling in negativity only perpetuates the cycle of low-energy vibrations.

Scientific research supports the notion of 'good vibes' and the impact of both high and low vibrations on our well-being. When we immerse ourselves in negativity and surround ourselves with others trapped in low vibrations, our own energy levels suffer. It becomes a self-reinforcing cycle, increasingly difficult to break free from. Conversely, when we actively seek out positive influences and surround ourselves with high-vibration individuals, we are more likely to experience an uplift in our own energy levels. Positive energy breeds creativity, motivation and a sense of empowerment, allowing us to tap into our full potential.

CHALLENGE

Who's in your immediate circle? Make the effort to seek out high-vibration connections and communities that nurture creativity, growth and fulfilment. Do an audit of your own self-talk. How much time do you spend fixating on the negatives, and how much on the positives? Write down one creative project you would go for or embark on if you weren't stuck in self-sabotaging thoughts.

DAY 15: CUT OUT THE EGO

Let's get real for a moment. What are you truly afraid of? Is it the fear of releasing your work and it not meeting expectations? Or are you afraid of everyone seeing it and getting crushed by the pressure of wild expectations you won't be able to top?

Your deepest fear should be that of not pursuing what you were born to do. Here's a list of things you can genuinely be wrong about: self-doubt, neglecting your art, procrastinating, giving up, speaking negatively about other creators, compromising your values to achieve success . . . The list could go on forever.

What's not on this list, though, is this: trying, evolving, improving, transforming, creating what brings you joy. Making sincere efforts to change perspectives. Anything you do with your whole heart is inherently beautiful. Stop fearing the unknown and embrace the journey of creative growth and self-expression.

CHALLENGE

Write down a mistake you've made in your creative work, whether it was pushing for something or stopping halfway through the project because of your insecurities. What did it teach you? How would you handle it differently in the future?

DAY 16: IT'S GOING TO HAPPEN

This creative journey you're on – it's not just a hobby or a passing phase. It's a calling, a purpose that you're meant to fulfil with every fibre of your being.

Eat it, breathe it, sleep it – immerse yourself fully in the creative process. Dedicate yourself wholeheartedly to your craft and you will see the fruits of your labour. Nobody can promise you exactly what success will look like, but you can rest assured that if you keep going, you will find your place in this world.

Keep pushing forward, keep creating and keep believing. The work is not in vain. It's a beacon of hope and possibility for everyone who dares to dream. Through your art, you will create purpose, ignite passion and unlock possibilities – not just for yourself, but for others as well. This journey isn't just about you; it's also about the people who may find solace and inspiration in your work.

CHALLENGE

Let creativity lead instead of control. When you're done, don't judge it – just let it exist. See what happens when you create purely for the sake of creating.

DAY 17: BE THE BUTTERFLY

Artists and butterflies are cut from the same cloth. We are summoned to undergo a transformative process, much like the metamorphosis of a caterpillar into a butterfly. This journey often leads us into periods of isolation, where we delve deep within ourselves to distil every life experience into something uniquely our own.

Yet, this cocooning period is far from glamorous. It's a constant struggle, a wrestling match with our identity, our message, our voice and our ultimate destiny. We yearn for the breakthrough, the moment of emergence from our cocoon as a fully formed artist. But here's the twist: the breakthrough isn't the end goal.

True artistry lies not in the finished product but in the relentless devotion to the process itself. We must embrace the cycle of creation, destruction and transformation. It's a perpetual journey of becoming, a continuous loop of birthing butterflies only to return to the cocoon and repeat.

Being an artist is a calling to engage in the perpetual breakdown and reconstruction of life itself. In this process, we find beauty, meaning and purpose.

CHALLENGE

Reflect on your progress and get excited about what lies ahead. Journal about your journey so far – note your current thoughts and feelings and come back to it whenever you need to remind yourself that these challenges are temporary, and you will get your breakthrough.

DAY 18: GOOD THINGS HAPPEN WHEN YOU TRY

You're emerging from a low point in the creative cycle – the phase where you feel beaten down and unable to lift yourself up. But now, you sense a glimmer of hope as the sun begins to rise over the horizon. It's time to give it another shot. This is when you reconnect with your childlike energy, that boundless enthusiasm and optimism. Push yourself to maintain a positive outlook, to see the glass as half full. Just give it a try. You can do anything you want. You are bound by nothing.

CHALLENGE

Set aside 15 minutes to do something you loved as a child, whether it's drawing, playing a simple game or exploring nature. Focus on the joy and freedom you felt in those moments.

DAY 19: TELL THE STORIES ONLY YOU CAN TELL

The world doesn't require perfect conditions to witness the brilliance of your talent. What it craves is your raw, unfiltered expression – the genuine essence of who you are. It's time to shatter the walls of excuses and embrace the imperfections that make you uniquely you.

Your art deserves to be seen, to be experienced, to be felt. It's a reflection of your soul, a manifestation of your innermost thoughts and emotions. And only you hold the key to set it free into the world.

So let go of the fear of imperfection. Embrace the authenticity of your craft and allow your true self to shine through. Your art is a gift waiting to be shared with the world.

CHALLENGE

Set a timer for 10 minutes and write a raw and unfiltered account of something that happened to you in the past year. The story can be as simple as an encounter at a petrol station or as significant as the best piece of news you received. Write from your perspective, and let your thoughts flow naturally, focusing on the emotions and details that made the experience uniquely yours.

DAY 20: TENDING YOUR CREATIVE GARDEN

Creativity doesn't bloom under pressure. It needs space, sunlight and patience. Like a garden, your creative life will have seasons – times of growth, times of rest, and times when things fall apart so something new can take root. You can't force it. But you can tend to it. Protect it. Show up for it every day, even when you don't see immediate results. The real work is learning to care for it long enough to watch it grow.

CHALLENGE

Identify the 'weeds' in your creative garden – distractions, doubts or anything else that clutters your creative space. Write these down and consider ways to address or remove them.

DAY 21: TAKE UP SPACE

Please, stop making yourself so small. Please, say out loud that you are an artist and your voice is worthy of being heard. Your art is worthy of being seen and you are worthy of taking up some space on this big rock. This is the idea that will take you to that breakthrough you are so desperately seeking. The old you who didn't do the things you were supposed to is trying to claw back through your soul. Tell that part of you to go back to sleep. This is your moment. You are no longer making things up. You are walking in your calling and it's time you owned it. This is not smoke and mirrors. This is real. You are real. Your art is real.

CHALLENGE

Today, make an effort to say out loud, 'I am an artist, and my voice is worthy of being heard. My art is real and it deserves to take up space.' Repeat this affirmation until you feel its truth resonate within you.

DAY 22: GIVE YOURSELF THE CHANCE

This is your moment. The wave has come. It's time to surf or drown. Creativity does not wait. It doesn't wait for the perfect moment, the perfect conditions or the perfect inspiration. Instead, creativity fashions its own perfect moments out of imperfect ones. It's about seizing opportunities, taking risks and pushing forward with unwavering determination.

You've worked too damn hard to get here, to let this moment slip away. This is your time to press in at all costs, to embrace the challenges and to fully commit to your creative vision. It's about trusting in yourself, trusting in your process and trusting that breakthroughs are not only possible but inevitable when you dare to push beyond your comfort zone and reach for greatness.

CHALLENGE

Reflect on a creative project or idea you've been hesitant to start or share because you didn't feel ready. What's holding you back? Is it fear of failure, lack of experience or other doubts? Take a concrete step towards making it happen, even if it feels imperfect or risky. Draft an outline, share your idea and set a deadline.

DAY 23: GET BACK TO CREATING

The stagnant, stale energy swirling through your body is no one's responsibility but your own. Once you're done feeling sorry for yourself, it's time to get started. Creating and repeating. Sometimes we get stuck in the repeating part. It's time to force yourself back into creation mode. Create not only art but a new life and perspective for yourself.

Let's get fresh air pumping back through your bones. This will revitalize you. It's time to activate!

Face yourself and recognize your power to change direction. Embrace new experiences, new sights and new flavours. Let this invigorate your creative spirit. By confronting yourself, you can break free from the patterns holding you back and step into a world brimming with possibilities. Reignite your passion and let your creativity flow. The journey begins with you.

CHALLENGE

Switch up your routine to embrace new experiences. Take a different route to work, try a type of coffee you've never had or listen to a genre of music you've never explored. Let these new sights, flavours and sounds invigorate your senses and inspire your creativity. Use this fresh perspective as a catalyst to start a new creative project or revisit an old one with renewed energy.

DAY 24: TRUST YOURSELF ALREADY

To fully embrace your inspiration and take a leap of faith, you must trust yourself completely. Accepting yourself as you are is crucial to initiating change and embarking on the creative process. This journey is continuous, with cycles of growth and transformation.

It's easy to be drawn to the idea of achieving widespread success. However, true artistry lies in creating for the love of the craft, with the intention of inspiring even just a few individuals. This process, driven by passion and authenticity, is where the true essence of art resides.

CHALLENGE

Reflect on a time when you doubted yourself but still took a leap of faith. What was the outcome? Write a short note to yourself about why you create and keep it visible as a reminder to trust in your journey.

DAY 25: DO WHAT YOU WANT TO DO

Doing what you truly want isn't just a luxury – it's essential to creating your best work. It might sound simple, but it's the foundation of every great breakthrough. When you chase what excites you, what sets your soul on fire, you create from a place of authenticity, and that energy is undeniable.

Let your passion be stronger than your fear. Fear will always try to hold you back – fear of failure, of judgement, of the unknown. But the desire that brought you here, the vision that keeps tugging at you, is more powerful than any doubt. You are not here to follow someone else's blueprint. You are meant to carve your own path, to trust the instincts that have guided you this far.

Everything in your life has led you to this moment, to this opportunity to create something only you can. Don't wait for permission. Don't wait for the perfect time. **Now is the time.** Step forward, trust yourself and bring your vision to life. The world is waiting for what only you can offer.

CHALLENGE

Set a timer for 2 minutes and jot down as many things as you want to do. They don't have to be just creative projects; include things like trying a new restaurant, changing your hair colour or visiting a country you've been curious about.

DAY 26: SUPPORT YOUR CREATIVE FRIENDS

Today is the day. Support is not always a two-way street, but let's understand something important: being a supportive friend to another artist is the *Create.Repeat* way. If any one of your friends, colleagues or acquaintances is doing anything that takes courage, you should show them love and support.

Withholding support from others is ultimately withholding it from yourself. If you think that won't affect other areas of your life, you are mistaken. If you want flow in your life, you need to give flow. Being that friend who freely gives praise and encouragement when it's deserved is a beautiful thing.

Remember, supporting others doesn't diminish your own accomplishments. Instead, it enhances your sense of connection and fulfilment. When you give freely and generously, you invite the same energy back into your life. Be the friend who cheers others on, who gives flowers when flowers are due. Spread confidence and positivity wherever you go.

CHALLENGE

Today, make an effort to comment, like and support your friends who are putting themselves out there. It's not easy to take risks and be vulnerable, especially in today's world. If you can be the reason someone gains confidence, you should be.

DAY 27: YOU ARE HAPPENING TO TIME

One of the most fascinating experiences is the moment just before something beautiful happens – a pause filled with anticipation, nerves and gratitude. In these moments, time stretches out and you truly see yourself. Life isn't just happening to you; you're actively engaging with it. These moments are rare, so savour them.

Write down how you feel during these times. Remember who you are before your big project takes off, as these are the moments that shape your journey. Often, we worry about not having enough time, but these perceptions can be illusions. Embrace the stillness and anticipation; they are the foundations of your artistic life. By appreciating these moments, you realize you are an active creator of your experience.

CHALLENGE

Reflect on a recent moment of anticipation before something significant happened. Write down your thoughts and feelings during that time. Set aside 10 minutes to sit quietly and observe your surroundings and emotions. Embrace the stillness and appreciate the process.

DAY 28: HONESTY IS FOR YOU

Being honest in life, honest in your art, and just plain honest is not overrated. Honesty is not primarily for other people; it is for you. Honesty sets you free. When you confront the things in front of you, you move past them. You no longer have to carry them with you.

Avoiding the truth and lying to yourself is like strapping a heavy backpack onto your shoulders. Imagine carrying a 30-kilogram backpack around an airport – no one enjoys that. So why do it metaphorically?

By embracing honesty, you shed that unnecessary weight. You stop burdening yourself with the things you're avoiding. This liberation allows you to move through life with more ease and grace. It's not about facing the truth for others' sake but for your own well-being and growth.

Honesty clears the path for authenticity and true self-expression. When you are honest, your art and your actions reflect your genuine self. This authenticity resonates with others, but more importantly, it resonates within you. It aligns you with your true self, fostering a sense of peace and freedom.

CHALLENGE

Be honest today.

DAY 29: DON'T SAVE THE HARD STUFF

Every artist needs dedicated technical office hours. While we might spend days floating in the creative ether, there comes a point when we must come down to attend to emails and communicate with clients.

Creative organization is crucial because it builds a structured environment that supports sustained creativity and ensures your creative flights are grounded in reality, which is essential for artistic endeavours. Timely communication and maintaining visibility through updated portfolios, social media and networking opens doors to new opportunities and partnerships.

Attitude is everything. How we approach these necessary tasks determines our success and the frequency with which opportunities arise. By embracing these moments with a positive attitude, you ensure that your creative flights are well-supported and that you can continue to soar. Art is not just about talent, hard work or luck; it's about the attitude you bring to every aspect of your journey. So, welcome these tasks with open arms and watch how they elevate your artistic career.

CHALLENGE

Tackle one administrative task you've been putting off, whether it's responding to emails, updating your portfolio or organizing your workspace. Approach it with a positive attitude, seeing it as a necessary part of your creative journey.

DAY 30: ACTIVATE

This word. ACTIVATE. To set something in motion or to start it up. There's immense power in this word. Reflect on what it means to you. Notice how it feels to say it – the way you have to move your mouth to pronounce it. Just like speaking it, creating the world you envision requires you to move your body, mind and soul.

Activation doesn't have to be a grand gesture. It can be as simple as picking up the phone and telling a trusted creative that you have a stirring in your soul. It's about taking that first step towards bringing your idea down to earth. Don't be intimidated by this word. Let it energize and inspire you. Activation is about progress, no matter the scale. It's about moving from point A to point B, one small action at a time.

Today, embrace the power of activation. Allow it to feed your spirit and propel you forward. Trust that each step you take, no matter how small, brings you closer to your dreams.

CHALLENGE

Take a small, actionable step today to set something in motion – whether it's starting a new project, reaching out to a creative friend for collaboration or simply organizing your thoughts and plans.

DAY 31: PLAYING IT SAFE

The greatest version of yourself is dormant inside your soul. Stop numbing your passion to avoid disappointment. We will say that again: stop numbing your passion to avoid disappointment. Numbing takes the pain away temporarily, but it doesn't eliminate it. If you ignore your dreams, they're still pulsing through your veins.

Playing it safe all the time doesn't always keep you safe. Your creative soul is in danger when you constantly put it on mute. That muscle desperately needs to be exercised. It needs to be used. It can never be taken from you but imagine the growth that can happen in a year of practising versus completely ignoring the parts of yourself that make you feel most alive.

Feeling alive doesn't always mean feeling good. It means feeling – experiencing the full spectrum of emotions. To feel is to be alive. Whether you're sad, in pain, happy or celebrating, you need all the colours of your emotional palette. Embrace every emotion, as they all contribute to the richness of your creative journey.

CHALLENGE

Identify an area in your creative life where you've been playing it safe or holding back. Today, take a step out of your comfort zone and take a risk. Embrace the full spectrum of emotions that come with it and allow yourself to grow from the experience.

DAY 32: SURRENDER TO THE PROCESS

Let go of the need for perfection and trust that each step, no matter how small, is part of your unique creative evolution. Dive into the flow and find joy in the act of creation itself. In surrendering to the process, you unlock the freedom to innovate and the courage to express your true artistic vision.

Perfectionism imposes rigid constraints, while letting go of it unlocks creative freedom. This freedom allows you to push boundaries, break rules and explore new creative territories. It empowers you to express your artistic vision without self-imposed limitations.

The pressure to be perfect can lead to stress, anxiety and burnout. By letting go of this pressure, you create a healthier and more sustainable creative practice. You become kinder to yourself, more patient with your progress and more appreciative of your achievements.

CHALLENGE

Choose a creative task or project and approach it with the mindset of surrendering to the process. Focus on the act of creation itself, rather than striving for perfection. Allow yourself to experiment, make mistakes and explore new ideas without judgement.

DAY 33: CONFIDENCE IS A PRACTICE

CONFIDENCE – this word needs to stop feeling icky. This word is power, and as artists, it's something we need to embrace fully. What do you have to lose by having unshakeable self-belief? It's easy to assume that confidence comes naturally to some people. But just like creating and repeating, confidence is a practice. It's something you can learn and reinforce every single day. Right now is our chance to redefine this word. Let confidence and the feelings it brings change the way you see the world and create within it.

Confidence isn't about showing everyone how comfortable you are with yourself. It's for you. Be courageous *for you*. Be fearless *for you*. Be unstoppable *for you*. When you make that adjustment solely for yourself, it starts to seep into the beautiful things you make and share with the world. Be an artist *for you* and make things that make you happy. When you create from that space inside, you enter a whole new altitude. That is something to truly believe in. That's authenticity, and that's beautiful.

CHALLENGE

Take a piece of art, a story or a song that you love and reimagine it in your own style. This could mean rewriting a classic story, covering a favourite song with your own twist or reinterpreting a famous painting.

DAY 34: ONE OF THOSE DAYS
YOU WILL TALK ABOUT

Maybe today is the day you'll reference on that podcast or talk show as part of your come-up story. Today, you're living that day. You are running into the red of your bank account, and it feels impossible to believe you can create a life out of this hole. Let us tell you how: one day at a time.

You are better today because you've made it through your hardest challenges. You are better today because that's what YOU choose to be. What you get to create today is your attitude. How you carry yourself when life is at its lowest point matters. Champagne problems or not enough money for Champagne problems are still problems. You get to choose what you see. Don't let the lust for more blind you and prevent your art from happening today.

Today, what is happening is: this book. You are reading something that comes from one of those days for us. But we choose to be here with you and continue the relentless pursuit of *Create.Repeat.*

That strength builds the best kind of art – the art that comes from struggles and shapes you into the incredible person you are.

CHALLENGE

Decide how you want to carry yourself and your attitude. What positive action can you take, no matter how small, to improve your situation?

DAY 35: BRAVERY NOT REQUIRED

The brave don't lead the brave; the willing do. It's not always the most talented, the most artistic or the luckiest who win. It's the most consistent. Success goes to those who want it the most and who never give up.

In any endeavour, it's the willingness to show up, put in the effort and persevere through challenges that truly sets people apart. The brave may have moments of courage, but it's the willing who persist day in and day out. They are the ones who, despite setbacks and failures, keep moving forward with determination and grit.

Consistency is the key to unlocking potential and achieving success. It's the relentless pursuit of goals, the daily commitment to practice and improvement that builds mastery and excellence. Talent can give you a head start and luck can provide opportunities, but without the willingness to work hard and stay dedicated, these advantages can fade away.

The willing are those who embrace the journey, understanding that progress is often incremental and success is a marathon, not a sprint. They cultivate habits that sustain their efforts, finding motivation in the small wins and learning from the losses. Their unwavering dedication becomes their greatest strength, outlasting those who rely solely on natural ability or fortunate breaks.

CHALLENGE

Focus on consistency. Create a plan or schedule to hold yourself accountable and ensure you show up every day.

DAY 36: THE WAY KNOWS THE WAY

The way knows the way. You can't force it; the way unfolds naturally, guiding you towards what is destined for you. Trust that the path will reveal itself in due time. Your role is to show up, stay present and keep moving forward, step by step. Each day, put one foot in front of the other, and you will find that the way is always leading you to exactly where you need to be.

Embrace the journey, knowing that the way has already mapped out your destination. The countless beautiful little things that had to align perfectly for you to be where you are right now are nothing short of miraculous. You are not a mistake, and everything bubbling up within your chest right now is right on time. Let the feelings of doubt and displacement push you to step forward. Trust in the way, and let it carry you to your destined placc.

CHALLENGE

Release the doubt.

DAY 37: MANIFEST A FEELING

What feeling do you want to feel? Art evokes emotions and your soul needs that nourishment. How you get there, what you create and how you share it are all important aspects of the journey. But what's most important is imagining the feeling.

If you feel stuck, go to this place of emotion and work backwards. Your imagination is the most powerful tool you possess. On a brain scan, reality and imagination look almost identical. This means that by vividly imagining the feeling you want your art to evoke, you can begin to manifest it into reality.

Visualize the joy, the connection, the impact your art will have. Picture the satisfaction of creating something that truly resonates with others. Let these imagined feelings guide your creative process. Your imagination is not just a playground for ideas; it's a wellspring of potential. Use it to water the seeds of your creativity. See the colours, hear the sounds, feel the textures of your imagined masterpiece. Let these sensations drive your work.

Remember, the art you create is an extension of the feelings you conjure within. By focusing on the desired emotions, you can channel your energy and creativity into making art that truly moves you and others. Manifest the feeling, and let your imagination transform it into reality.

CHALLENGE

Take a moment to visualize the feeling you want your art to evoke.

DAY 38: FACE YOURSELF AS AN ARTIST

Stuck in time. Having to wait. Nothing else to distract yourself with. Now what? You can't do anything but face yourself. Remember those little wind-up toys that walk straight into a wall and keep hitting it until you change their direction? That's you. The hardest truth sometimes is realizing that no one but yourself can readjust your course. Only you can make that pivot.

If you want change, go after it. If you want to be a new version of yourself, just start. You need to use your senses again. You need to see something new on your way to that 9 to 5 that is draining your soul. Paint your world again with fresh colours and shake things up.

CHALLENGE
Switch it up today. Do something different. Pivot.

DAY 39: STAY TRUE

As an artist, perception can be a tricky thing. It's easy to get caught up in how others see you or what you think they expect of you. But here's the truth: none of that really matters. What truly matters is staying true to yourself and honouring what calls to you creatively.

In the world of art, authenticity reigns supreme. It's about expressing your unique voice, embracing your vision and creating from a place of genuine passion. Whether others understand your work or not, whether they praise it or criticize it, is secondary to the joy and fulfilment you find in the creative process itself.

Remember, art is deeply personal. It's about exploring your inner world, pushing boundaries and making sense of the world around you through your own lens. What matters most is that you are being true to your artistic vision, following your instincts and creating from the heart.

So, let go of the need for external validation or fitting into others' expectations. Focus instead on nurturing your creativity, exploring new ideas and letting your artistic journey unfold naturally. Trust in your intuition, embrace your unique perspective and let your art speak for itself. In the end, staying true to yourself is the most powerful statement you can make as an artist.

CHALLENGE

Wear the outfit that best represents the most authentic version of yourself. Notice how it influences your confidence and mindset. By aligning your external appearance with your true self, you'll likely feel more empowered and at ease. This simple act can reinforce your self-expression, boost your creativity and remind you to stay true to your unique vision.

DAY 40: DEEP COMMITMENT

Hatred and pain are two distinct experiences, especially when it comes to your art and yourself. You don't hate your art; rather, your relationship with your creative vision can sometimes be fraught with pain. There are days when your artistic journey feels challenging, when doubts creep in and when the creative process itself becomes a source of struggle.

It's important to recognize that this pain is not a reflection of hatred towards your art or yourself. Instead, it's a natural part of the creative process – a reflection of the passion, intensity and emotional investment you pour into your work. This pain can stem from striving for perfection, grappling with self-doubt or confronting the vulnerability of artistic expression.

Embracing this pain means acknowledging the depth of your commitment to your craft. It's a sign that you care deeply about your art, that you're willing to push boundaries and that you're open to exploring new depths of creativity. This journey isn't always smooth or easy, but it's where growth happens, where breakthroughs occur and where your artistic voice evolves.

CHALLENGE

Find an old project that caused you frustration or difficulty and spend 15 minutes revisiting it with a fresh perspective. Before diving in, write down one positive aspect of the piece and one challenging aspect. Then, try an unconventional approach: change the medium, alter the style or introduce a new element. Use this exercise to explore the boundaries of your commitment and see how you can transform pain into creative growth.

DAY 41: REMEMBER WHERE YOU CAME FROM

The person you are today is someone you once dreamed of becoming. In our creative world, who you are in this moment holds immense significance. There were days when you longed for clarity and pursued your aspirations with unwavering determination.

Now that you're here, embrace this version of yourself. Reflect on the journey that brought you here – the challenges overcome, the lessons learned and the growth experienced. Remember the passion that fuelled your dreams and the persistence that propelled you forward. Let your past achievements inspire you to continue pushing boundaries, creating boldly and evolving as an artist. Honour your journey, for it has shaped the artist you are today and will guide you towards the future you envision.

CHALLENGE

Write a letter to your younger self, focusing on the dreams and aspirations you had back then. Describe how you've grown, the challenges you've overcome and the skills you've developed. Include advice and encouragement based on what you've learned.

DAY 42: YOU DON'T KNOW EVERYTHING

If having all the knowledge meant having everything, wouldn't you already have it all? Instead of pretending to know everything, embrace being a student again. Ask questions, be curious. This is where creativity flourishes most. It's inspiring and refreshing to witness someone else's process unfold before you. Remember, no one can replicate what you create with your unique soul. So, release the need for control and simply observe. There's so much to gain from letting others take the lead.

Also, remember this: if you find yourself in the role of teacher, sharing your knowledge generously doesn't diminish your own creative power. There's abundance in creativity; we don't have to be gatekeepers. The energy you put into sharing and teaching will come back to you in positive ways. Embrace the cycle of creation and sharing. Let the wave of fresh perspectives and ideas wash over you repeatedly, enriching your own creative journey.

CHALLENGE

Take a step towards learning by sending a cold email or DM to someone whose creative process or skills you admire. Express your genuine curiosity about their journey and ask if they'd be willing to share some insights or advice. Be open and respectful and remember that it's okay if they don't respond – what matters is that you took a leap today. Reaching out and seeking knowledge is a valuable step in your creative growth.

DAY 43: ENJOY THE RIDE

As the rollercoaster reaches its peak and the exhilarating drop is imminent, hold on tight and savour every single moment. These are the days we've eagerly anticipated and diligently worked for. This moment makes all the challenges and struggles seem insignificant in comparison. This wild ride won't last forever, so it's crucial to relish every joyful second.

As artists, we're often conditioned to brace for the next setback. But what if we trained ourselves to fully embrace these moments of success as opportunities to live in the present? You can acknowledge the hardships later; for now, let the thrill of achievement activate you and soak in every ounce of gratitude possible. You've earned this! This moment is a testament to your consistency and dedication. You're not an imposter; you're an artist who crafts incredible stories. Embrace this high – it's well-deserved.

CHALLENGE

Create a 'Victory Jar' where you write down your recent accomplishments, big or small, on slips of paper. Decorate the jar and place it somewhere visible. Today, add a note about a recent success, detailing how you felt and what it means to you. On challenging days, revisit the jar to remind yourself of your achievements. This physical representation of your victories will serve as a tangible reminder of your progress and dedication, helping you savour and celebrate each high point in your creative journey.

DAY 44: WASTE OF TIME

Is there really such a thing? Every experience informs the next. Reflecting on all the endeavours we embarked on before *Create.Repeat* came to be is humbling. The DNA of *Create.Repeat* carries strands from each of those projects and experiences. So, if you feel like your current job or daily tasks are a waste, they are not. The only waste is maintaining a negative attitude. How you fold that shirt or crunch those numbers for a client directly influences how you approach your art on difficult days when inspiration feels elusive. Practise your mindset now. Focus on seeing opportunities rather than obstacles and cultivate a positive approach that will strengthen your creative practice in all circumstances. Every moment contributes to your growth as an artist – nothing is truly wasted.

CHALLENGE

Choose a seemingly mundane task you do regularly, like cooking, cleaning or a work-related activity. As you perform this task today, focus on doing it mindfully and with intention. Pay attention to any thoughts or ideas that arise. You might find inspiration or solutions for a project you're working on.

DAY 45: SHOOT YOUR SHOT

You have not because you ask not. How can you rewrite your story today? Think about someone in your life. Whether it's an old friend, a loose connection or someone you admire from afar. Chances are there's someone you've been meaning to reach out to. But for some reason, you haven't. Why? What do you truly have to lose? Let go of trying to be too cool for it. Your future hinges on these moments. Whether it's seeking answers, offering your help or taking a chance on a project that could transform your life – why hold back from something with that potential? Even a small change can make a significant difference. You need fresh perspectives, and you hold the keys to unlock the doors standing before you.

CHALLENGE

Write down a list of five people or opportunities you've been thinking about but haven't acted on. Choose one and take a small but concrete step towards it today. It could be sending a message, applying for a grant or pitching an idea. As you do this, reflect on any fears or hesitations you feel, and remind yourself that growth happens outside of your comfort zone. Embrace the unknown and take your shot – you never know what doors might open.

DAY 46: EVERY PART OF YOU MATTERS

Sometimes we feel sadness. It can be disheartening to realize that the artistic expression we've cherished for so long needs to evolve as we move through different stages of life. Sometimes it feels like change shows up unannounced, asking us to let go of old versions of ourselves as artists. But does this mean we've vanished? No, we believe not. Instead, it marks a time of evolution – a period for our art to retreat into its cocoon and emerge renewed. Like a caterpillar transforming into a butterfly, our creativity undergoes a metamorphosis, revealing fresh and thrilling forms of expression. This reinvention isn't an end, but a beautiful beginning – a journey of exploration and growth that guides us to new artistic horizons.

Your new journey has begun. You've found a way to express yourself and thrive in one season of your life. Now, as the season changes, it's time to discover a new creative home and way of life. This is the essence of life as a professional creative – constantly adapting, evolving and finding innovative ways to share your unique voice with the world.

CHALLENGE

Reflect on how your artistic expression has evolved over time. Look at how far you've come.

DAY 47: FIND HOME

Feeling at home in your own body can be challenging. There are days when you wake up and forget what timeline you're on. That's okay. As creatives, we are constantly dreaming of what is to come, pulling things down from the clouds that don't exist here on Earth. This is no easy feat. We are astral projecting ourselves to other places to create works of art. Our message to you today is to get grounded. Find the tether that pulls you back down to Earth and give yourself grace.

You may be off in the clouds, floating, but use your senses and remind yourself that you are where your feet are planted. Dissociating can be a survival tactic, but right now, you need to associate with every aspect of your life. Understand that every facet of your mind is necessary for where you are going. Today, you are holding this book, reading this page. You are here. Breathe. We will never get this day back.

We promise you that you've got this. You have everything you need right inside of you.

CHALLENGE

Choose a simple grounding activity, such as walking barefoot on grass, sitting quietly in nature or holding a small object that brings you comfort. As you engage in this activity, focus on the sensations and allow yourself to be fully present. This exercise will help you connect with your physical self and the world around you, finding a sense of 'home' within.

DAY 48: CREATE BECAUSE YOU HAVE TO

Draw upon something greater than yourself for inspiration today. Perhaps it's your family, who have fought so hard to create the home they have today. Maybe it's a mentor or someone you look up to. Or maybe it's deeper – honouring the legacy of the millions of artists on whose shoulders we stand.

Work today from a place of honour. Honour the artists who redefined colours, shapes, shadows and how we see art. Think of the iconic filmmakers, actors, painters, sculptors and writers who paved the way for us. We create today because of them. How beautiful is it to acknowledge their sacrifices, especially in a time when creating was not as easy as it is today? These people did not create out of convenience; they created because they had to, driven by an unquenchable fire within their souls.

Today, channel that same energy. Create because you absolutely have to.

CHALLENGE

Make something. Anything.

DAY 49: BUILD A FENCE AROUND THE PLAYGROUND

When you're feeling stuck and aimless, the problem might be too many options. For creatives, endless possibilities can sometimes be paralyzing. That's when it's time to build a fence around the playground.

Giving yourself constraints forces you to change your approach and focus on what truly matters. Once that fence is built, you're free to explore within those boundaries. This structure provides a playground where you can innovate and express yourself without feeling overwhelmed.

Within this space, you can experiment, take risks and push your creativity – whether it's going down the slide, around the merry-go-round or up the climbing frame. The key is to stay within the playground's boundaries; this doesn't limit your artistic expression but rather channels it, sometimes requiring you to colour within the lines. Constraints can foster creativity, helping you to find unique solutions and refine your work.

CHALLENGE

Identify a current project or creative idea that feels overwhelming due to too many possibilities. Set specific constraints or rules for yourself – such as limiting your colour palette, using only certain materials or setting a time limit. Work within these boundaries today and see how they help you focus and channel your creativity.

DAY 50: BE OPEN TO FEEDBACK

Creativity thrives on feedback – it's integral to growth and progress. Whether you're an artist or navigating life, feedback is essential, even if it's challenging at times.

It's crucial to listen not just to solutions but also to the underlying problems. Sometimes, we're too close to our work to see the issues clearly. Feedback offers fresh perspectives that can lead to creative breakthroughs. Remember, feedback isn't personal. It's about improving your work, not criticizing you as a person. Don't let it discourage you; instead, use it as a tool for improvement.

We all have moments of defensiveness, but being open to feedback means approaching it with an open mind. Take what resonates with you and consider how it can elevate your work. Discard what doesn't align with your vision or values.

Ultimately, feedback is a pathway to refinement and growth. Embrace it as a constructive force that helps you evolve creatively and personally.

CHALLENGE

Share a current project with someone you trust and ask for their honest feedback. Listen carefully to their insights, focusing on understanding their perspective rather than defending your work. Write down the feedback and reflect on how it can help you improve your project. Remember, this is an opportunity to grow and refine your skills. Take what resonates and consider how you can incorporate it into your work.

DAY 51: SHOOTERS SHOOT

Don't let the pursuit of perfection stifle your creativity. Embrace the flow of ideas, let your imagination soar and capture the essence of your inspiration without overthinking. Some of your best work comes from allowing ideas to flow freely and passionately. You're holding on too tightly. Loosen your grip and get your practice in. Stop being overly cautious and immerse yourself in the creative process. Remember, shooters shoot, right? It's a numbers game at this point. You need as many shots as possible.

Keep creating and stay prepared for those moments of brilliance. Allow your creativity to unfold naturally, trusting that each idea contributes to your growth and artistic journey.

CHALLENGE

Today, set aside a specific amount of time to create without any restrictions or overthinking. It could be 30 minutes or an hour – whatever works for you. The goal is to let ideas flow freely and capture them without worrying about perfection. Whether you're writing, drawing, composing or any other creative pursuit, focus on producing as much as you can in that time.

DAY 52: PLAYTIME

Start playing again. Start dreaming again. Remember why you began this journey. At some point, a light switch flipped off inside your soul. You listened to someone else, let feedback silence you and allowed comparison to steal your joy. That light switch is still inside you, waiting to be flipped back on. Remember when you were free and let your imagination run wild? Remember how happy it made you?

You can control that light switch. Find the power to flip it back on today. You are worthy of creating beautiful things with your whole self. You don't need to turn off parts of your brain to be your best. When you harness all of yourself, you'll feel that creative flow again.

CHALLENGE

Reconnect with your inner child by revisiting a creative activity you loved as a kid. It could be building something with blocks, finger painting or even playing an imaginative game. Allow yourself to immerse fully in this playtime, without worrying about the outcome.

DAY 53: CREATIVITY IS NOT HINDERED BY STORMS, IT'S BORN FROM THEM

Whatever has you feeling wrapped up and beaten down right now, know that you will make it through. If you feel lost . . . GOOD. Being lost means you're on the path to being found. You can only get answers by asking questions.

You've been doing the same thing the same way for too long. If you want a different result, it's time to embrace being lost again. The storms swirling around you, both physical and metaphorical, are signs that change is coming. And it's for the better. Life and art are not meant to be static. They are meant to shift, evolve and give birth to new experiences. So, surrender to the storm. Embrace what scares you and have faith in yourself. Trust that your feet will find solid ground again.

CHALLENGE

Reflect on a challenging time you've faced recently or in the past and write about how it affected you and what you learned from it.

DAY 54: DEEPLY FEELING HUMANS

Don't beat yourself up today. Being a deeply empathetic artist is both a blessing and a curse. To create beautiful art, we must feel deeply. But sometimes, being so connected to those around us interferes with our creative process. The best thing we can do is be aware of this. Notice how others affect you during the week and be selective about who you let in. Protect your creative flow from outside influences.

Remember, who we are today is shaped by many layers, including how our younger selves survived in this world. Sometimes, it's not as simple as just sitting down and getting to work. Maybe today, you need to honour those layers. Acknowledge your triggers, feelings and the empathy that flows through your heart. It's the best part of you and the reason you are a creative.

CHALLENGE

Feel your feelings today.

DAY 55: YOU CAN CHOOSE TO FAIL

You can put your energy into something safe and still face failure – so why not take a chance on what truly excites you? It's a powerful realization: no path is guaranteed, so the best investment you can make is in something that fuels you. This isn't about rejecting stability or walking away from a 9 to 5. It's about making sure that, whatever you do, your creativity isn't left behind. Whether you're in a boardroom, a classroom, a studio or working on a side project after hours, your time and energy should go towards something that brings you alive.

If what you're doing now inspires you, keep going. If it doesn't, give yourself permission to explore, to create, to build something that does. You don't have to choose between security and creativity – you just have to choose to honour what truly matters to you.

CHALLENGE

Before you continue on your current path, ask yourself: is this truly what I want? If not, it may be time to recalibrate and pursue what truly ignites your soul. Journal about what you desire and what you wish to avoid in life. Reflect on your life's inventory to discover what truly brings you joy in your creative work.

DAY 56: BETRAYAL

Stop betraying yourself. When we think of betrayal, it often feels like a monumental act – sharp and heavy. But it exists in subtle, everyday moments. When you promise to find a vocal teacher to elevate your craft and then don't – betrayal. When you downplay something you love by calling it a 'little dumb project' – betrayal. Each time you're not true to yourself, to your passions, and to the world you want to create, you accumulate these small betrayals, leading to a significant breakdown.

Why do that to yourself? It's time to reclaim your creativity and stop the cycle of undermining your craft. Don't shrink yourself or compromise your authenticity just to make others comfortable. You deserve to show up fully as who you are.

CHALLENGE

Identify one small way you've been betraying yourself – whether it's neglecting a project, downplaying your talent or putting off a goal. Take one bold step today to honour that part of you. Sign up for the class, share the project or simply call it what it is: meaningful. Show up for yourself.

DAY 57: DO IT FOR SOMEONE ELSE

From the second you wake up, you know what kind of day it will be. This morning, creativity comes knocking at 5 a.m. The grogginess and tired disposition are nowhere to be found. Heart is pumping and today is going to be different. This life as a creative is just constantly switching the sunglasses. Everything is the same, yet everything is entirely different because of how we see it. Tap into the quiet, still morning and remember why you started all of this. Where are you creating? Why are you creating? Who are you creating for?

If you can't do it for yourself today, remember those people – the ones who inspired you to see the world differently, who helped shape your perspective. This perspective can be so exhausting at times, but it is a life worth living. A life full of meaning and reasons behind it. You make the meaning. You make the art. You are the vessel. How lucky are you?

CHALLENGE

Reflect on the people who inspire you to create – whether they're loved ones, mentors or artists you admire. Spend a few minutes thinking about how your work can impact them or honour their influence.

DAY 58: OLDER, WISER

Getting older as a creative is a gift. It's an opportunity to rediscover your passion and creativity, to reconnect with what makes you special and uniquely you. As we age, we get new opportunities to find the spark again.

Remember the pure bliss of being a child, when imagination and play were natural? As we grow up, we might find ourselves in jobs we don't love, feeling disconnected from that creative spirit. But ageing gives us the wisdom to revisit those passions with a new perspective and appreciation.

Embrace the journey of growing older. Rediscover your creativity. Rekindle the joy of what makes you, you.

CHALLENGE

Reach out to the oldest person you know – whether it's a grandparent, mentor or coworker. Spend some time talking with them and ask for their advice or insights on life, creativity or any challenges you're facing. Soak up their wisdom and perspective. Use this conversation to reflect on the value of experience and the lessons they can offer you as you continue your creative journey.

DAY 59: IT'S UP TO YOU

We are alive. We woke up and we are breathing. What a gift it is to simply be alive! No matter what is coming today or what happened yesterday, we have this singular moment. What do you smell? What do you hear? And what is your soul saying to you today? Don't let what's happening on your phone distract you or tell you that you are not doing enough. Today, by simply waking up and picking up this book, you have done something for yourself. Maybe you build on that today? Maybe you rest? It is up to you.

CHALLENGE

Spend a few minutes in a quiet place, away from distractions, and listen to what your soul is telling you. Reflect on your goals, desires and what truly matters to you. Then, set one intention for the day that aligns with these reflections – whether it's taking time for self-care, pursuing a creative project or reaching out to a loved one. Remember, it's up to you how you choose to spend this day.

DAY 60: IT WILL MAKE SENSE LATER

For this moment, trust and believe that everything will work together for your ultimate good. All the random activities and opportunities coming your way are leading you to a greater purpose. Nothing is wasted. Every experience adds to the foundation you're building. Sometimes it feels like you're caught in a whirlwind, doing so much and feeling like all roads lead to unpaid work. But day by day, it will begin to make sense. Keep putting one foot in front of the other. Clarity is coming, and defining what you do should be the last worry on your mind. Just keep swimming.

CHALLENGE

Create a visual representation, like a vision board or a simple collage, of where you want to be in the future. Include images, words and symbols that resonate with your goals and dreams. As you work on this, remind yourself that each small step and seemingly random opportunity is guiding you towards this vision. Keep this visual reminder somewhere you can see it, and trust that your path will make sense in time.

DAY 61: UNDER A BUSHEL

Embrace the quiet, unseen work – it's the foundation for your brightest moments. Our ego craves visibility, recognition and applause, but this desire can often distract us. Some of our most authentic and powerful work happens when we're in a hidden space, away from the spotlight. Though our ego resists, our creative soul thrives in these moments of solitude. The time spent out of view, crafting your song, painting your art or developing your next project, is a precious gift. Keep your light under the bushel until the time is right to shine. It's in the quiet, unseen work that your true brilliance is nurtured.

CHALLENGE

Spend time today working on a creative project without sharing it publicly. Focus on the process rather than the outcome or recognition. Allow yourself to enjoy the quiet, unseen work and reflect on how these moments contribute to your growth and authenticity as an artist. Remember, some of your most meaningful work happens away from the spotlight.

DAY 62: GET AS UNCOMFORTABLE AS POSSIBLE

Want to work as a professional creative? You'll need an entirely different level of endurance to make it. You won't always be working on your own creative clock, and that's good for you. You have to build up stamina.

As a creative, you know you won't always get to do things your way. You must be willing to collaborate, and in this space there's room for growth and expansion. A creative hobby and a creative job are two very different methods of working. Embrace the discomfort – it's a sign that you're pushing boundaries and evolving. The road to greatness is paved with challenges, and it's through these trials that your true potential is revealed.

So, get uncomfortable. Push yourself beyond the familiar and watch as you transform your creative passion into something extraordinary.

CHALLENGE

Identify a skill or area of your creative work where you feel less confident. Spend at least 30 minutes today focused on developing that skill, whether it's through practice, research or seeking feedback from others. Embrace the challenge and acknowledge any discomfort as a necessary step in your growth. Keep a journal of your progress and any breakthroughs you experience, as this will help you track your journey and see the value in pushing your boundaries.

DAY 63: TO BE OR NOT TO BE

To be or not to be? To be creative or to not? Both are hard, both are unknown and both are a risk. This echoes Hamlet's contemplation of existence: enduring life's hardships ('to be') or escaping through the unknowns of death ('not to be'). As a creative, you face similar dilemmas in your journey. Embrace your existence, your creativity and your purpose. Stand confidently in your truth, knowing that your work and passion are meant to be shared. Don't shy away from opportunities or doubt your worth. You are here to create, to inspire and to leave a mark. Be present, be bold and be unapologetically you.

CHALLENGE

Choose a quote or passage that resonates with your journey as a creative person. Write it down and place it somewhere visible as a daily reminder of your purpose and passion. As you go about your day, repeat the quote to yourself whenever doubts or uncertainties arise. Let this mantra help you stand confidently in your truth and embrace the challenges and rewards of your creative path.

DAY 64: CREATE BECAUSE YOU LOVE IT

When was the last time you created just for the joy of it? Not for a deadline, not for a goal – just for the love of making something. Loving what you do is electric. But as we get older, fun isn't always encouraged the way it used to be. We get caught up in routines, prioritizing what makes money or supports others, often forgetting to make space for what truly makes us happy.

But what about you? What about the things that light you up? Do more of that. Shift time to work for you. Because when you create from a place of joy, you show up as your best self – you laugh more, live larger and have even more to give to the people you love.

Creating for the love of it is one of the strongest forms of self-care. Let yourself enjoy it.

CHALLENGE

Spend 15 minutes brainstorming or sketching out an idea you've always wanted to explore. It doesn't matter if it's a big or small project – just let your imagination run wild. If you can't create it today, write down your thoughts and ideas, describing what it would look like and why it matters to you.

DAY 65: ADD FUEL TO THE FIRE

Today, we're not letting a single moment pass without stepping into the life we want to live. This isn't just another day; it's *the* day. The day you'll look back on as the turning point. Everything you're seeking and striving for is already within you. All it takes is sitting down and doing the work.

Don't let the technicalities or fears hold you back. Today, we're embracing a mindset where everything you touch turns to gold. Every idea, every creation, every business concept is a home run.

Dedicate time to your passions and pour fuel on your creative fire. This is the day you commit to creating and repeating until you're living your dreams. Make it happen.

CHALLENGE

Choose a project you've been working on and take it to the next level. Whether it's adding a new element, refining your work or expanding its scope, commit to amplifying your efforts today. Spend 15 minutes brainstorming ways to elevate your project, then dive in and execute one of those ideas. Treat today as the day you fan the flames of your creativity and make a significant leap forward. Let this be a day of action and transformation.

DAY 66: SPEAK WITH PURPOSE

Every word that leaves your lips carries weight – especially when it comes to the creativity and art you share with the world. It's no longer just a project; it's your expression, your essence laid bare. If you can't speak positively about the art you're creating, reconsider your words. Your subconscious absorbs every doubt and uncertainty. Be kind to yourself. Convince your sensitive artist's soul that you are unique, brilliant and worthy of your dreams. Your voice matters – start by believing in it yourself.

CHALLENGE

Watch how you speak about yourself and your work today. Notice any negative or doubtful thoughts and consciously reframe them into positive affirmations. Speak with purpose and kindness, reinforcing your belief in your unique voice and creativity.

DAY 67: SET YOUR IDEAS FREE

Set your ideas free from the confines of your mind; don't let them fade into silence. Every creative spark deserves to be nurtured and brought to life. Take action without hesitation, embracing the thrill of manifesting your ideas. Allow them to grow, evolve and inspire. Your creativity is a gift meant to be shared with the world – let it extend beyond your imagination. Embrace the liberation of expressing your authentic self, transcending any fear of judgement.

CHALLENGE

Set aside 15 minutes to brainstorm and jot down every idea that comes to mind, no matter how big or small. Don't censor yourself or worry about feasibility – just let your imagination flow. Afterwards, pick one idea and outline a simple plan to start working on it. This exercise will help you free your creativity and take the first steps towards bringing your ideas into reality.

DAY 68: COMPARISON KILLS CREATIVITY

Navigating comparisons among creative friends can indeed be challenging, especially in a bustling creative city where everyone seems to be chasing their dreams. It's crucial to prioritize your own journey and goals amidst the achievements of others. Celebrate your unique path and personal milestones, consciously stepping away from social media comparisons and nurturing appreciation for your own creativity. Genuine support for each other as sources of inspiration, rather than rivals, fosters a healthier community dynamic. When feelings of comparison arise, practising self-compassion is key – we're all human, susceptible to doubts and insecurities.

Remember, this community of artists is essential; throughout history, artists have thrived by supporting each other. By cultivating a supportive environment and focusing on personal growth, we can navigate comparison and flourish creatively together.

CHALLENGE

Take a break from social media today, or even for the entire week. It's good for you.

DAY 69: GET SERIOUS

Today is dedicated to mapping out your creative journey with clarity and purpose. Goal setting isn't just about envisioning where you want to be; it's about crafting a roadmap to get there. Begin by reflecting on your aspirations – what sparks your passion, what ignites your creativity?

Write them down, breathe life into them with ink on paper and let them take shape beyond your thoughts.

Equip yourself with tools for progress tracking – a journal, a calendar or digital apps – to monitor your growth consistently. Track not only your achievements but also the lessons learned from setbacks. Every stroke of the brush, every written word, every captured moment is a testament to your dedication and resilience.

As you embark on this journey, remember: creativity thrives in the space where ambition meets action. Today, set your goals high, track your progress diligently and let each step affirm your commitment to creating and evolving. Your artistic vision is unique – nurture it, guide it and watch it unfold beautifully throughout the year.

CHALLENGE

Set up a weekly check-in system to monitor your progress towards your creative goals. Every week, review what you've accomplished, what challenges you've faced and what you've learned. Adjust your plans as needed and celebrate even the smallest victories. This regular practice will help you stay on track and maintain momentum in your creative journey.

DAY 70: EMBRACE

Today, we celebrate the artistry that surrounds us in the ordinary – the rhythm of daily life, the unnoticed beauty in routines. Creativity isn't confined to grand gestures or special occasions; it flourishes in the small moments, in the mundane, waiting to be discovered by those with eyes open to possibility.

Pause to observe the world around you: the patterns of light filtering through the window, the melody of raindrops on the roof, the dance of colours in a bustling street. Each moment holds a story, a spark waiting to ignite your imagination. Embrace these simple moments as seeds for creativity.

Incorporate creativity into your daily rituals – whether it's sketching during your morning coffee, finding poetry in your commute or capturing fleeting moments with your camera. Engage with the world as a canvas, where every interaction, every thought, can be transformed into something uniquely yours.

CHALLENGE

Today, focus on finding beauty in the ordinary moments of your day. Take time to observe and appreciate the small details around you, whether it's the way sunlight falls on a surface, the sounds of your surroundings or the interactions you witness. Capture these moments through a quick sketch, a photograph or a few written lines. Embrace artistry in the everyday.

DAY 71: SABOTAGE

We often undermine our own efforts without any external help. As artists, we constantly bring new, innovative creations into existence, yet maintaining confidence can prove to be our greatest challenge. It's a practice that extends beyond our creative endeavours – it's about embracing every step of our journey, regardless of where it leads.

Even if what you're creating right now isn't exactly what you envisioned, it's still a step forward and a manifestation of your passion and creativity. Embrace and share it proudly because every piece of art you produce has the potential to bring joy and inspiration to others. Recognize the beauty in this process and honour the impact your work has on those who encounter it.

CHALLENGE

Take a moment to identify any self-sabotaging thoughts or behaviours that might be holding you back. Write them down and then counter each one with a positive affirmation or action you can take to overcome it. For example, if you wrote, 'I'm not good enough to finish this project,' counter it with, 'I have the skills and creativity to bring this project to life.' Acknowledge that every step you take, no matter how small, is progress. Celebrate your achievements, even if they don't perfectly match your original vision, and recognize the value in each creative effort.

DAY 72: HEALING POWER OF CREATIVITY

Grant yourself the liberating gift of unravelling and processing your emotions through art. Let creativity be your trusted companion on this journey of self-discovery and healing. As you engage in the act of creation, give voice to your innermost thoughts and feelings, finding solace and inspiration in every brushstroke, word written or melody composed.

Confronting and releasing difficult emotions as they surface is pivotal – this moment is yours to face them bravely and transform them into artistic expression. Remember, your mental well-being is fundamental to your creative path. By nurturing your mind and creating space for clarity, you cultivate an environment where creativity thrives effortlessly.

A clear mind is the canvas upon which your creativity paints its most profound stories. As you embrace this journey of emotional exploration, allow yourself the freedom to delve deeper, ensuring your artistic expression flows authentically and with boundless inspiration. Today is a testament to your courage and creativity – may it lead you to new levels of artistic discovery and personal growth.

CHALLENGE

Do whatever you need to do to clear your mind today. Whether it's going for a walk, meditating, journalling or simply taking a break from your usual routine, focus on activities that help you relax and find clarity. Use this time to recharge and reconnect with yourself, knowing that a clear mind is essential for your creative journey.

DAY 73: ADVOCACY

Harness the power of your art to advocate for the causes that resonate with you. Your creativity can amplify voices, raise awareness and inspire action on issues that matter deeply to you and the world. How beautiful is it that we have the power to do this? This is why being creative is a calling. Art transcends barriers and ignites change, making it a powerful tool for advocacy. Remember, your perspective is valuable. By expressing your convictions through your craft, you contribute to a larger dialogue and encourage others to think, feel and act. Your art can be a catalyst for progress, sparking conversations and fostering understanding.

Embrace this role of artist-advocate with passion and purpose. Today, let your creativity be the bridge between your heart and the world, transforming your art into a powerful force for advocacy and impact. Your voice matters and, through your art, it can make a profound difference.

CHALLENGE

Reflect on how your creative skills can contribute to advocacy. Spend time today brainstorming ways you can use your art to support a cause – whether it's through collaborating with nonprofits, creating art for awareness campaigns or organizing an event. Write down your ideas and set a small, achievable goal to start working on one of them. Remember, every step you take helps amplify the impact of your advocacy and supports the causes you care about.

DAY 74: SAFE IS BORING

You're not doing anything special if you're not scared. Changing the way people see the world shouldn't feel like a safe, cosy feat. It should feel fiery and exciting.

When you step into the unknown, pushing the boundaries of your creativity, fear is a natural companion. Embrace it. Fear means you're venturing into uncharted territory, challenging norms and daring to make a difference. It's in these moments of discomfort that the most impactful and revolutionary art is born.

Think about the artists, innovators and visionaries who have shaped history. They didn't play it safe. They took risks, faced their fears head-on and created work that disrupted the status quo. This fiery energy fuelled their passion and propelled them to create art that changed perspectives, sparked movements and inspired generations.

CHALLENGE

Think of a creative risk you've been avoiding because it feels too challenging or uncertain. Commit to taking that risk today. It could be sharing your work with a new audience, experimenting with a different medium or tackling a controversial topic. Document your feelings and the process and reflect on how taking this leap makes you feel. Celebrate the courage it takes to embrace fear and pursue something bold and meaningful.

DAY 75: IT WILL BE WORTH IT

Hold on to the vision. Trust in your process and know that every setback is just a setup for a greater comeback. The world needs your unique voice, your perspective, your art. There will come a time when you look back on these days and see them for what they were: the crucible in which your creativity was forged.

Keep pushing forward, keep believing in your talent and keep creating. It will all be worth it. The world will see, feel and be transformed by what you bring into it. And in that transformation, you will find your own fulfilment, knowing that you dared to dream and had the courage to make those dreams a reality.

CHALLENGE

Repeat this affirmation to yourself: 'I am capable, resilient and my creativity has value. Every step I take brings me closer to my dreams.' Say it aloud or write it down, and keep it in a place where you can see it throughout the day.

DAY 76: BELIEVE

Believe in the power of your creativity to make a difference. Your unique perspective and talents have the potential to inspire, heal and transform. When you feel overwhelmed, remember that even the greatest masterpieces were born from moments of doubt and uncertainty. Trust in your vision and your ability to bring it to life.

Keep pushing forward with passion and determination. Surround yourself with people who uplift and inspire you and seek out experiences that ignite your imagination. The road may be long, but each step you take brings you closer to your dreams. In the end, you will look back and see that every challenge, every setback and every triumph was worth it. Your creative journey is a gift to the world, and it will shine brightly, lighting the way for others to follow.

CHALLENGE

Write down a list of three specific reasons why you believe in your creative abilities. Reflect on past achievements, moments of inspiration or feedback from others that affirmed your talents. Keep this list somewhere visible as a reminder of your potential and the power of your creativity to make a difference.

DAY 77: RIDE THE WAVE

Creativity ebbs and flows like the tides. There are moments when inspiration hits you like a powerful wave and you feel unstoppable. In those moments, it's crucial to drop everything and ride that wave. Embrace the surge of energy and ideas, let it carry you, and create with abandon.

Being a seasoned creative means understanding that these highs don't last forever. The initial rush of inspiration is intense but fleeting. Make the most of it. When you're in the flow, immerse yourself fully in your work. Allow the ideas to pour out without overthinking or second-guessing. This is the time to experiment, take risks and push the boundaries of your creativity. When the wave recedes, don't be disheartened. The quiet periods are just as important. These moments of calm are when you can evaluate your work, refine your ideas and set new intentions for your creative journey.

CHALLENGE

Be mindful of any surge of inspiration you feel today. If you sense that creative energy building, take note of what sparked it. Whether it's a piece of music, a conversation or a new environment, try to recreate or stay in that moment to keep the inspiration flowing. Engage in an activity that fuels your creativity and see how long you can ride the wave. Document the experience and reflect on what helps sustain your creative momentum.

DAY 78: ACCEPT THE 'L'

The 'L' is the loss. Today might not be your day. Don't fight it – some days are just scheduled losses. It's not personal. Embrace the moment, try something different and let yourself be. Sometimes, that's all you need.

CHALLENGE

Give yourself permission to step away from the pressure to create and focus on self-care. Remember, it's okay to have an off day.

DAY 79: TODAY IS A GREAT DAY TO START YOUR PASSION PROJECT

What's a project you've always wanted to do but haven't started yet? This question holds a special place in the heart of every creative person. It's that lingering idea, the one that excites and terrifies you in equal measure. It's the project that you dream about, the one that lives in the back of your mind, waiting for the perfect moment to come to life. It could be a business venture, a new invention or a collaboration with someone you admire.

This project, this dream, represents the purest form of your creative potential. It's untouched by the constraints of time, fear or doubt. Yet, it remains unrealized, often because we tell ourselves we're not ready, that we don't have the time or that it's too ambitious.

But what if you started today? What if you took the first small step towards making that project a reality? The journey of a thousand miles begins with a single step, and the same is true for your creative dreams. Starting doesn't mean completing it all at once. It means committing to the process, embracing the uncertainties and allowing yourself the freedom to explore and grow.

CHALLENGE

Spend 15 minutes today brainstorming and outlining your passion project. Write down what excites you about it, what you hope to achieve and any potential challenges you foresee. Break the project down into smaller, manageable steps and set a realistic timeline for each phase.

DAY 80: BE OPEN

History repeats, creating the future. Throughout history, artists have consistently reinvented themselves and their craft. Their evolving methods, groundbreaking innovations and diverse inspirations offer a treasure trove of ideas for us to explore and adapt in our own creative journeys.

Are you inspired by trying new methods? Perhaps stepping into a different character's shoes could offer a fresh perspective. Could a weekend immersed in reading ignite new ideas? Or might you challenge yourself like Stephen King by committing to write 2,000 words daily, regardless of the circumstances?

Embrace the opportunity to experiment and push your boundaries. By integrating new approaches into your creative process, you not only honour the legacy of those who came before but also pave the way for your own future innovations.

CHALLENGE

Explore the work of an artist or creator you're not familiar with or delve deeper into a lesser-known piece by one of your favourites. It could be a movie you've never seen from your favourite director, a B-side track from an artist's early work or a book from an author outside your usual genre. Watch, listen or read with an open mind.

DAY 81: PERMISSION TO EXPLORE

Let's take a page from David Bowie's book. His extraordinary ability to reinvent himself and embrace various personas throughout his career serves as a powerful reminder for all creatives: exploration and evolution are vital. Why are you clinging to a single approach or identity? What's holding you back from seeing beyond your current self? You generously offer advice, perspective and grace to those around you. But what about yourself? How can you give yourself permission to explore and experiment?

Imagine the possibilities if you allowed yourself to delve into something entirely new. What if you began as an actress and discovered a passion for writing? Why should that journey be seen as anything other than a thrilling exploration of your creativity? Your career does not define who you are. It's your soul, your joy and your willingness to evolve that truly shape your identity. Embrace the freedom to reinvent yourself and explore new facets of your creativity.

CHALLENGE

Take some time to watch interviews with David Bowie. Pay attention to how he speaks about his creative process, his willingness to experiment and his embrace of different personas.

DAY 82: PATIENCE IS NOT INACTION

Patience is often misunderstood as passivity, but in reality, it's a dynamic and active force. It's not about waiting idly or resigning to fate; it's about staying engaged and committed while the process unfolds. Embracing patience means continuing to work, refine and grow, even when results aren't immediate. It's about maintaining your focus, nurturing your goals and trusting in the journey, knowing that every step you take contributes to the bigger picture. So, let patience be your active ally, propelling you forward with purpose and perseverance.

CHALLENGE

Reflect on a current project or goal where you feel impatient for results. Write down the steps you've taken so far and acknowledge the progress you've made. Remind yourself that growth takes time and that each step is valuable. Today, commit to a small, intentional action that supports your long-term goal, and trust that your patience will pay off in the end.

DAY 83: EMBRACE YOUR NEW PATH

You belong somewhere, even if it's not where you've always been. Stop beating yourself up and convincing yourself you've failed. The world is full of unpredictable events that have nothing to do with you, so if your career or life goals aren't unfolding as planned, see it as a sign, not a setback. Use this moment to push forward with renewed determination. Every twist and turn is a result of your effort, guiding you towards new possibilities. Remember, the push you give will pave the way, and the way will reveal its own path. Embrace the journey and trust that it's leading you exactly where you need to go.

CHALLENGE

Take time to reflect on an unexpected change in your life or career. Write down how this change has opened up new possibilities or taught you valuable lessons. Set an intention to approach your current situation with a positive mindset, focusing on the opportunities it presents rather than the challenges.

DAY 84: STAY IN IT

Stay in the game. It might not feel like it today, but inspiration has a way of showing up when you least expect it. Remember the story of the gold miners who gave up just three feet from striking gold? They had dug and toiled for miles, only to abandon their efforts right before their breakthrough. The lesson? Keep going. Your breakthrough might be just around the corner. Trust that your efforts are leading you closer to the gold you seek. Stay persistent, stay in it and let inspiration find you as you keep pushing forward.

CHALLENGE

Keep going.

DAY 85: BE LIKE MIKE

Michael Jordan's journey to becoming a legend wasn't without its setbacks; he was famously cut from his high school basketball team. Instead of giving up, he used this as motivation to work harder. Jordan practised relentlessly, honing his skills and pushing his limits, which eventually led him to become one of the greatest basketball players of all time.

Jordan often talks about how he's missed more than 9,000 shots and lost almost 300 games. He failed over and over again, but he used each failure as a lesson to improve. This mindset is crucial in pursuing a creative life as well. Embrace every challenge and setback as opportunities to learn and grow. Like Jordan, let your passion drive you to practise tirelessly, refine your craft and approach your work with a champion's mindset. Your creative greatness isn't just about talent; it's about the commitment and grit you bring to your craft.

CHALLENGE

Identify a recent setback or failure in your creative journey. Reflect on what you can learn from this experience and how you can use it to improve. Write down three specific actions you can take to refine your skills and overcome this challenge. Embrace the mindset of continuous improvement and use this opportunity to push your creative boundaries further.

DAY 86: ADAPTABILITY IN SUCCESS

Here's your golden nugget as a creative: adaptability in achieving success is the secret ingredient that transforms challenges into opportunities. It means being able to adjust and refine your approach, strategies or methods in response to ever-changing circumstances and new obstacles. Adaptability is your superpower. It allows you to thrive in dynamic environments, pivot when necessary and continually evolve your craft. Embrace this trait and let it guide you through the twists and turns of your creative journey. Adaptability is not just about surviving; it's about flourishing amidst change and turning uncertainty into your greatest asset.

CHALLENGE

Take some time today to explore a new tool, technique or genre related to your creative work. Step outside your comfort zone and try something unfamiliar, even if it feels challenging. Reflect on how adapting to new methods or ideas can open up new avenues for creativity and success. Use this experience to remind yourself that being adaptable not only helps you overcome obstacles but also enhances your overall growth and potential.

DAY 87: BE HERE

Sometimes it feels like it takes everything just to get to this moment. Why is that? Why does it feel so hard to do the things you know you need to do? It's exhausting – constantly fighting resistance, feeling weighed down by the past, by expectations you've carried for so long. But maybe it's time to let go. Let go of what you think you should be doing or who you think you need to be. All you need is today – this moment, right now. Be at peace with yourself, with your body, with your life, just as they are today. Not focused on what they'll become. You are grateful. You are present. You are here. And that's enough.

CHALLENGE

Deliberately focus on a part of your process that feels repetitive or unglamorous. Make it the highlight of your day – whether it's sharpening pencils, adjusting lighting or preparing materials. Find beauty and value in the routine acts that build your creative practice.

DAY 88: TAKE CREATIVE RISKS

Innovation often requires reimagining traditional formats and taking creative risks. The Beatles are a perfect example of how daring to be different can lead to extraordinary results. From their early days, The Beatles were unafraid to experiment with their music, pushing boundaries and challenging norms. Their embrace of psychedelic sounds, unconventional recording techniques and elaborate concept albums set them apart from their peers and reshaped the music industry.

One of their most significant risks was the creation of *Sgt. Pepper's Lonely Hearts Club Band*, an album that defied traditional structures and incorporated a diverse array of styles, from orchestral arrangements to avant-garde elements. This move not only redefined what an album could be but also cemented their legacy as pioneers in creative experimentation. This is why their music feels timeless.

Embrace your own creative risks with confidence! You know that stepping out of your comfort zone can lead to groundbreaking achievements and profound personal growth. So DO IT! Your willingness to take risks can forge new paths and shape your creative legacy.

CHALLENGE

Listen to *Sgt. Pepper's Lonely Hearts Club Band* by The Beatles.

DAY 89: POWER IN COLLABORATION

Collaboration is a powerful catalyst for innovation and creativity, transforming individual efforts into something greater. Think of iconic collaborations like John Lennon and Paul McCartney, whose partnership in The Beatles produced timeless music, or Steve Jobs and Steve Wozniak, whose synergy built Apple from a garage startup to a tech giant. These partnerships show that when people come together, they blend unique skills and perspectives, leading to extraordinary results.

Effective collaboration is more than just working alongside others; it requires a genuine openness to different ideas and a willingness to combine strengths. By embracing diverse viewpoints and talents, you can push creative boundaries and achieve innovations that might be impossible alone.

Let this be a reminder to actively seek out and value collaboration in your creative journey. Whether it's partnering with someone in a different discipline or simply brainstorming with a friend, the synergy that comes from working with others can elevate your work and open doors to new possibilities. Don't shy away from collaboration; embrace it as a vital part of your creative process.

CHALLENGE

If you're not already working with a collaborator, now is the time to seek one out. Look for someone who complements your skills and strengths, especially in areas where you might be weaker. A creative partner can offer fresh perspectives, enhance your ideas and hold you accountable.

DAY 90: EVOLVE OR DIE

The willingness to evolve is a powerful trait that distinguishes great creatives from the rest. It's not just about adapting to change – it's about embracing it wholeheartedly and using it to propel your craft forward. Evolution requires you to face new challenges. It forces you to experiment with new ideas and continually push the boundaries of your creativity.

This dynamic process of evolution allows artists, writers and innovators to stay relevant and impactful. It fosters growth and leads to breakthroughs that might not be possible without stepping into the unknown. Through this constant evolution, many have achieved their most profound and enduring contributions.

Remember, evolution isn't optional; it's essential. Embrace change, adapt with intention and let the journey of evolution guide you to new heights in your creative endeavours.

CHALLENGE

Reflect on how you can evolve in your creative journey. Consider exploring new technologies, genres or styles you've been avoiding. Start thinking outside the box and envision yourself in a new light. With the next season approaching, take this time to prepare and embrace the opportunities for growth and innovation that lie ahead.

DAY 91: MAKE WHAT SCARES YOU

The best work you'll ever create isn't the easiest – it's the work that makes your stomach drop. The idea that feels too risky, too vulnerable, too real. The one you keep pushing aside because it feels like too much.

So why do we avoid it? Because making something honest means there's no excuse. No hiding behind trends, algorithms or what's 'safe'. Putting yourself into your work means there's a chance it won't be understood. But it also means it could be the thing that finally connects.

Some of the most groundbreaking creative works came from artists following what felt true, not what was expected. Donald Glover refused to stay in one lane, bouncing between comedy, music and film. Phoebe Waller-Bridge turned a small, deeply personal stage play into *Fleabag*, a cultural phenomenon. Bo Burnham started with goofy YouTube videos and ended up making *Inside*, a raw meditation on art, the internet and mental health.

None of them were waiting for the perfect idea. They just started. And they made what scared them.

CHALLENGE

Think about the project you've been avoiding. The idea that feels too big, too personal, too real. Start it today. Even if it's messy. Even if it's just a single sentence. Move towards the fear, not away from it.

DAY 92: BE BOLD

Say something. Actually, say something. We know it's scary to share your opinion with the world, but you need to be reminded that there is power in your perspective.

Being bold doesn't mean being loud or abrasive; it means having the courage to express what truly matters to you, even when it goes against the grain. It means trusting in your vision and being willing to share it, knowing that not everyone will agree, but understanding that those who resonate with it will find strength in your words.

So, what is your truth? What do you stand for? What do you want to challenge, change or celebrate?

CHALLENGE

- Reflect: Take a few moments to reflect on the issues, ideas or experiences that are most important to you. What have you been hesitant to express and why?
- Express: Choose one of these topics and create something around it – a piece of writing, a painting, a song or any form of expression you prefer. Focus on conveying your true feelings and thoughts, without holding back.
- Share: If you feel ready, share your creation with others. Whether it's through social media, a blog or a close circle of friends, put your bold statement out into the world and embrace the vulnerability that comes with it.

DAY 93: DO NOTHING

You read it right. Creatives need days where you let your brain flat-line. This is your excuse to rest and recharge.

CHALLENGE

Rest.

DAY 94: ELEVATE EMPATHY

Perhaps your speciality isn't in elevating your art through the latest technology but through the power of your heart. Empathy-driven creatives have a unique ability to shape the world not just by what they create, but by how they connect with and understand those around them.

Think of empathy as the core of your creative practice. It's about seeing and feeling the world through the eyes of others, particularly those who need love and understanding the most. By allowing your heart to guide your work, you bring a profound depth and resonance that technology alone cannot achieve.

Your creativity can become a powerful force for change when it's rooted in empathy. It allows you to address real needs, convey genuine emotions and create meaningful connections. Embrace this approach, and let your heart be the driving force that shapes your art and impacts the world.

CHALLENGE

Take a moment today to reflect on someone else – a close relative, friend or colleague. Consider their journey: their life, their struggles and their accomplishments. Reflect on how their experiences and achievements have shaped them and perhaps even influenced your own path.

DAY 95: COMPASSIONATE CREATIVITY

Fred Rogers, an American television host and a creative genius in his own right, showed audiences in the US that true brilliance often comes from leading with the heart.

Through *Mister Rogers' Neighborhood*, he demonstrated the power of empathy, authenticity and genuine connection. His ability to address complex emotions and make everyone feel valued and understood set him apart as a remarkable creative.

Let Mr. Rogers' story inspire you to infuse your own work with heartfelt empathy and sincerity. Lead with compassion, stay true to your values and create with the intention of connecting deeply with others. In doing so, you'll not only craft meaningful and impactful work but also touch lives in a way that resonates profoundly.

CHALLENGE

Find an old episode of *Mister Rogers' Neighborhood* on YouTube or a streaming service and watch it with fresh eyes. Let yourself be transported back to simpler times. You're sure to discover some timeless wisdom you can take to heart.

DAY 96: APPLAUSE WON'T KEEP YOU ALIVE

Artists vs. Tinker Bell. Are we the same? We would argue that, in some seasons, absolutely. Like Tinker Bell needing applause to stay alive, many artists thrive on the affirmation of others – the claps, the praise, the recognition that fuels their creativity. Let us guess: you feel undervalued. The special glow has worn off. No one is giving you constant affirmation or rounds of applause anymore.

Welcome. This is the heartbeat of being creative.

CHALLENGE

Create something today without sharing it publicly or seeking feedback. No applause, no likes, no validation – just you and your work.

DAY 97: CHRONIC CREATIVE PEOPLE PLEASERS

This passage is dedicated to our constant, chronic creative people pleasers. Burnout to the nth degree, anxiety skyrocketing through your chest 24/7. This is the curse of wanting everyone to be happy with you, your art and what you are making, so their world can go round. But have you given so much to their world that you lost your own?

Learning to protect your energy, to speak up and to say no isn't selfish – it's survival. It's the key to maintaining your creative spark and protecting your passion. Without those boundaries, the art you love will slowly become the burden you despise.

So, take a step back, honour your own needs and remember: your worth isn't tied to your output or the happiness of others. It's tied to the care you give yourself, to your ability to stay inspired and to the courage it takes to say, 'No, I need this time for me.'

CHALLENGE

Write down one recent time you said yes when you wanted to say no. How did it feel, and what would you do differently next time? Schedule 30 minutes this week for an activity that inspires you. Turn off distractions and honour this time for yourself.

DAY 98: BLIND SPOTS OR UNSEEN POTENTIAL?

This is not what you want to hear. Sometimes we might not always know what is best for us. We can walk through life with blind spots, unaware of the patterns or habits that no longer serve us. If you find yourself thrust into an unexpected season – whether it's a sudden change, a setback or a shift in perspective – maybe that's the universe's way of nudging you towards awareness and growth. These unexpected moments can feel disorientating and challenging, but they provide the necessary space for reflection. They force us to reevaluate our paths, our life choices and the things we truly value.

So, when life throws you a curveball, consider it an invitation to explore the depths of your own being. It's a chance to shed old skin, uncover hidden strengths and move forward with a clearer understanding of who you are and what you want. Trust in this process; it may just be the catalyst for the change you've been waiting for. Embrace the discomfort, for it is often where the most significant growth occurs.

CHALLENGE

Write about a recent unexpected change or challenge in your life. What habits, patterns or assumptions did it force you to reconsider? List three ways this experience could lead to personal growth or new opportunities, even if they aren't immediately clear.

DAY 99: BE THE CHANGE

Allow yourself the freedom to reinvent and redefine what being a creative means for you. If you feel stuck, let's shake things up. Sometimes, you have to be the change you want to see. You need to ignite things to move forward. This might mean switching up your outfits, experimenting with a new hairstyle or even rearranging your space.

Sometimes, changing things on the outside can provide a fresh perspective for what's happening on the inside. Embrace the possibilities that come with these shifts and remember that every new experience can reignite your passion and inspire fresh ideas.

So, take a deep breath, let go of any limitations and dive into the exciting adventure of becoming the creative you're meant to be. You don't have to play it so safe.

CHALLENGE

Pick one external change – wear an outfit you've never tried, rearrange a corner of your space. Don't overthink it, just change a little something today.

DAY 100: EMBRACE MILESTONES

Today marks a significant milestone – Day 100. It's a moment to reflect on your journey, celebrate your progress and recognize the growth you've achieved. Reaching this point is a testament to your dedication, resilience and creativity. Honour your accomplishments, no matter how big or small. Each step forward shows that you believe in yourself, and that is powerful.

As you move forward, make sure your days are purposeful. Whatever you choose to do, give it your all. If you take a break, take it fully. If you work and create, do it with complete dedication. Bold decisions leave no room for regret.

CHALLENGE

Celebrate reaching Day 100! Take a moment to reflect on your journey so far, acknowledging the growth and achievements you've made along the way. This milestone is a testament to your dedication and resilience.

DAY 101: MONEY MONEY MONEY

The topic of money can feel both suffocating and liberating for creatives. You need it to sustain your life and pursue your passions, yet the pressure can create a barrier between you and the art you love. When financial concerns take centre stage, it's easy to lose sight of the joy and purpose that initially inspired your creativity. The need to make a living can overshadow the very reason you started creating in the first place. Finding a balance is essential. Allow yourself to be honest about your financial needs while keeping your artistic vision alive. Embrace the notion that money can be a tool to support your creativity rather than a constraint. Focus on what truly matters – your craft, your message and the joy it brings you and others. Remember, your worth as a creative is not defined by your bank account but by the passion you pour into your work. So let the money flow, but don't let it drown out your voice.

CHALLENGE

Write down three ways money has positively impacted your creative journey (e.g. enabling new projects, learning opportunities or giving you time to focus on your art). Let this practice shift your mindset towards gratitude and see money as a tool, not a barrier.

DAY 102: BE DELUSIONAL

Just do something. Anything. Stop waiting for the spark or the push from somewhere outside yourself. You are the light in the bottle. We've been conditioned to search for inspiration beyond our own minds and hearts, but the truth is that everything you need is already within you. Consider this: how does anything on this Earth get sold? It starts with belief. What if today you embraced the idea that you have everything you need to move forward with your dreams? By investing in that kind of self-belief, you unlock a powerful force within you. Be delusional, be uninhibited, be YOU. With that mindset, you become truly unstoppable.

So, take that first step, however small.

CHALLENGE

Be bold and take one wild, uninhibited action towards your dream today – send that risky email, post that unfinished sketch or pitch the 'crazy' idea. Act as if you're already unstoppable and let the rush of doing ignite your next move.

DAY 103: RED LIGHT, GREEN LIGHT

Friendly reminder! Brake lights don't mean 'no'. They don't mean you're stuck or going nowhere. To see brake lights, you had to first get in the car and start moving. You're on a journey and those lights are just a signal to pause, not to stop forever. Sometimes we need those moments to slow down, to reflect, to breathe. You're still going somewhere – this is just a temporary pause before you continue moving forward. So, take that moment, and know that the road is still waiting for you.

CHALLENGE

Take 5 minutes to reflect on where you are in your creative journey. Write down one thing this 'pause' has taught you and one step you'll take when it's time to move forward again. Remember, the road is still yours.

DAY 104: INTENTION MATTERS

Intention. As creatives, we're made of so many layers. Our world is built on empathy, meaning and constantly piecing things together. Intention is like a channel – a space we have to keep pure if we want to create from that place where everything just flows. When we let our intention get diluted or contaminated, it changes everything. The more you create for attention, the less you'll have. The more you create for approval, the further it slips away. You'll end up chasing an unattainable, never-ending goal.

Create because you can't not create. Because you love it. Because of that teacher who gave you a safe space to grow. Create to build those safe worlds for others to live in. Your intention is at the heart of everything you do. You may not always see it, but when that part of you gets corroded, your entire project can slip away before you even realize it.

CHALLENGE

Write down the core reason why you create – what drives you at your deepest level? Then, craft a one-sentence mantra that captures this intention. Keep it somewhere visible to remind yourself to create from a place of love, not validation.

DAY 105: SUCCESS IS NOT ALWAYS GROWTH

We often equate success with growth, imagining that becoming a new version of ourselves is the sole indicator of our progress. But what if there's more to success than just the relentless pursuit of growth? Consider the moments of stillness, the quiet reflections and the small victories that may not come with grand transformations. Success can be found in the simple act of being present, in the relationships we nurture and in the joy we experience in everyday life. It's about honouring where we are right now, even if it doesn't align with the traditional markers of growth. What if success was also about acceptance? Accepting ourselves as we are – with all our quirks, flaws and strengths – is a powerful form of achievement. Sometimes, it's in these moments of acceptance that we find clarity and contentment, realizing that we don't always have to be in a state of expansion to feel fulfilled.

CHALLENGE

Take a moment to celebrate where you are right now. Write down three 'successes' from today – no matter how small – whether it's a kind interaction, a moment of calm or simply showing up for yourself. Reflect on how these victories bring joy and fulfilment without needing constant growth.

DAY 106: LOOK BACK

Look how far you've come. It took you so long to move past that thing that broke your spirit but now you're on the other side. The feeling of the world crumbling beneath you is still close, yet it feels so far away. The pain sits just beyond the glass. If you were to breathe on it, you'd see it there, but don't pick it back up – it no longer serves you.

The swirling doubts, the constant feeling of not being good enough for someone or something, it's all behind you now. You've risen above it. Whether you realized it or not, you're *above* it now. So, stay there. Nothing can bring you down.

CHALLENGE

Take 10 minutes to reflect on a past moment that once felt insurmountable but now feels distant. Write down how you've grown since then and what you've left behind. Keep this as a reminder of your resilience whenever doubts resurface. Stay grounded in your strength – it's your anchor.

DAY 107: DEFY THE ODDS

Today, you will defy the odds. Yes, you. You're going to tap into that part of yourself that refuses to accept no as the final answer. No more pushing things off until tomorrow. Your soul can't take another day of denial. Today, you will find a way – any way – to express yourself.

This is your moment to move forward, to push past hesitation and let the momentum build. Even the smallest step counts. Ready? Set? GO.

CHALLENGE

Take one bold step today towards a goal you've been hesitating on. It could be a tiny action – sending an email, starting a draft or brainstorming ideas – but it must be something you've been putting off. The goal is to build momentum, proving to yourself that you can and will defy the odds. Ready? Set? GO!

DAY 108: EVERYTHING, EVERYWHERE, ALL AT ONCE

We promise – this is where the good stuff happens. That *everything, everywhere, all at once* panic attack? That's where the rubber meets the road. This is the moment in the creative process where you start shaking the trees, and whatever falls out needs to go. What remains are the things you've truly nurtured and poured your heart into. The projects born from people-pleasing or distractions? Let them shake away.

Keep the main thing the main thing. The focus, the passion, the work that matters – *that* is what deserves your energy. When you strip away the noise, you're left with what's real, what's true and what's meant to be. This is how you find clarity, and this is where the magic happens.

CHALLENGE

Take 10 minutes to 'shake the trees' of your creative life. Write down everything you're working on, then circle the one or two projects that truly light you up. Cross out or set aside the rest for now – focus your energy on what matters most. Keep the main thing the main thing.

DAY 109: 6,789 EXCUSES

You don't feel like it today, right? You're tired? No creative itch? Here's a reality check: if you're waiting for the perfect moment, skip to the next day and come back when you're ready to hear it. Success doesn't go to the most talented – it goes to the people who push through cement-thick resistance *every single day*, for years on end. That's the real calling of an artist. It's not some lucky break. Luck favours the prepared. You've got to break down those walls of bullshit. We've all got 6,789 excuses running through our veins. It's been that way since the dawn of time, but let's be real – it's getting easier and easier to be lazy with all the distractions out there.

Snap out of it. Seriously. Get off your ass and be the artist you were born to be *today*. There's no magic pill, no 'perfect moment'. You create the magic by showing up, even when you don't feel like it. So do the damn thing.

CHALLENGE

Prove to yourself that action creates momentum, even when you don't feel like it. Show up and *do the damn thing*.

DAY 110: LEARNING FROM COLLABORATIONS

One bad experience with a collaboration is not all experiences. A lot of times alignment is an experiment. You won't always know something is the right fit or the wrong fit until you're in the middle of a project. Take a deep breath. Do your best to honour the project and get it done. Once you have figured that part out, now it's time to reflect. Are there some areas where you could have been better? Are there things that unfolded not because they were right, but because you were acting from insecurity or without clear intention? Recognize that each experience, even the difficult ones, contributes to your journey as a creative person. Embrace the lessons learned and let them guide you in future collaborations. Remember, every collaboration is an opportunity for discovery, and with each project you're honing your skills, clarifying your intentions and, ultimately, moving closer to your creative vision. So, don't let one setback deter you; instead, use it as a stepping stone towards deeper understanding and stronger partnerships in the future.

CHALLENGE

Identify one thing you'll do differently in your next project to ensure better alignment and intentionality. Use this reflection to move forward with clarity and confidence.

DAY 111: HEALING SUN

Today, the sun rises, peeking through the trees, casting its golden honey rays that melt down every alleyway in the city. The sunlight touches the grooves, stairs and pavement – elements of the city that often go unnoticed. But by simply existing, these places still get to feel the sun's warmth. Just like those hidden spots, you too deserve to feel the sun's embrace. No matter what you created in the past, what you're creating in the present or what you will do in the future, you are deserving of the sun. Remember, no amount of fame, money or success can replace that feeling of warmth and light. It's a reminder that you are human, with an inherent worth that needs no validation. So, allow yourself to bask in that sunlight, to soak in its warmth and to embrace the truth that you are worthy of joy and inspiration simply for being you.

CHALLENGE

Take 5 minutes today to step outside and feel the sun on your skin (or imagine it if it's cloudy). As you do, remind yourself: *I am worthy of warmth, light and joy, simply for being me.* Let this moment ground you in your inherent value, beyond any external achievements.

DAY 112: FIND YOUR 'F' WORD

Forget the usual 'F' word – today, it's all about FOCUS. As a creative, finding your focus should be as intense and intentional as anything else you chase. It's not just focus – it's flow. When you tap into both, everything shifts.

In this space, ideas come alive and inspiration feels like second nature. It's where your truest self emerges and your imagination runs wild without boundaries. What's stopping you? It's time to lock in, let go and create like your life depends on it – because in a way, it does.

CHALLENGE

Eliminate all distractions – put your phone on silent, close unnecessary tabs and immerse yourself completely. Let the flow take over and see what you can create when your focus is unwavering.

DAY 113: LET GO OF EXPECTATIONS

You can't predict exactly how it'll turn out. Not fully. But every day, small degrees shift everything. Have you ever imagined that moment when you 'make it', only to realize that half the people you expected to be there aren't? That's the reality – so much of what we envision is beyond our control.

What you can control is this very moment. The expectations of what's to come later? They're out of your hands and the more you try to hold on to them, the more elusive they become. Focus on the now – because this is the only part of the journey you can truly shape. What's ahead will unfold in its own time, but it's this moment that's real, and it's this moment where we get to choose what kind of artist we want to be.

CHALLENGE

Reflect on one thing in your creative journey that you've taken personally – whether it's a rejection, a missed opportunity or unmet expectations. Write it down, then reframe it by identifying the bigger picture it's a part of. Ask yourself: how does this moment fit into the greater vision I'm working towards? Let it go, and lock into the work you can control today.

DAY 114: ART IS NOT RANDOM

Distractions. We get it – really. The world is constantly pushing and pulling us in every direction. But here's the thing: your art isn't just going to happen randomly. You have to plan for lightning to strike. And here's the hint – it's not coming from the sky. *You* are the lightning. You decide when to strike. You have to foster those moments and be ready for them. Nothing is random – not even inspiration. Do you really think the biggest artists just wait around for a burst of creativity? Sure, they may have their flashes of brilliance, but they've learned how to *make* the moments happen. They show up, put in the work and create the conditions for that lightning to strike.

Your success isn't just a stroke of luck or a sudden spark . . . it's built through intention, preparation and consistent effort. So, stop waiting for some random moment of inspiration. Instead, take control: create the space for it, trust yourself and strike when you're ready.

CHALLENGE

Create your 'lightning jar'. Grab a notebook or piece of paper and write down three things that inspire you most – music, a place, an activity. For your next session, incorporate one of these elements intentionally to set the stage for inspiration. You're not waiting for lightning to strike; you're summoning it.

DAY 115: EXPRESS YOURSELF

Express yourself however you can right now. That's how you will get started. You're not always going to just get to make the movie, open an art show or have every single resource ready to go. What you do have is yourself. You have your imagination. You have your creative mind ready to see things differently and imagine how things can still come to life. Maybe today, it's brainstorming costumes for your dream feature film, something that demands incredible attention to detail. You need to meditate on that. The clearer you see those characters, the clearer the story becomes. Notice how focusing on the smaller parts of the big, scary project makes it feel less overwhelming. It's okay to feel that weight, but remember – you can break it down, piece by piece, day by day.

CHALLENGE

Imagine your big project as a puzzle. Today, focus on crafting just one piece. Sketch a prop, write a character's favourite line or create a playlist that sets the mood. Let this small detail become a spark that brings the whole vision closer, one inspired fragment at a time.

DAY 116: SHHHH!

Get really quiet today. You need to find that still voice within yourself – the one that knows the answers. It's in there; we promise. If you feel lost and unsure of which way to turn, trust that you know deep down what's right for you. Remember why you made the choices that brought you to this very moment, and now it's time to follow through. Your past choices come with consequences that we must face. So, face them, extend grace to yourself and reconnect with why you started this journey in the first place. Shhhhhh. Do you hear that? There you are.

CHALLENGE

Close your eyes, take deep breaths and ask yourself: *Why did I start this journey?* Write down the first thing that comes to mind. Trust that still, quiet voice within you.

DAY 117: CHASE *CREATE.REPEAT*

It's not personal. You know that feeling when you're alone on a Saturday night and it feels revitalizing? But then, two Saturdays later, it's the third time you've spent the night alone, and suddenly you feel like no one cares about you or your work, and that no one sees you for who you truly are. It's a spiral.

But what if you spent those Saturdays chasing something instead? Chasing the *Create.Repeat* of your life – whatever keeps you up at night. Become the graphic designer, the seamstress, the jewellery maker. You have everything you need; you just have to want it bad enough and carve out a little time to go all in. Remember, you have friends. This is just a season. Pour yourself into your project and when you look around later, you'll see how far you've come.

CHALLENGE

Dedicate your next Saturday night to chasing your creative dream. Choose one small, meaningful task – design a logo, sew a stitch, sketch a piece – and spend the evening fully immersed in it.

DAY 118: FORM THE HABIT

If you started doing something consistently every day for the next 2 months – drawing, writing, designing, whatever – you'd likely start to identify with it, right? So much can shift in just a few days without you even noticing. Our habits shape who we are, and they all begin on a random day we choose to start.

Today could be that day for you. The day you begin becoming the person you've always dreamed of being. A few days from now, you'll look back and realize you're no longer just aspiring – you're doing it. You're becoming the artist, the creator, the doer. One step at a time, you're already on your way.

CHALLENGE

No matter how simple or imperfect, choose to keep the momentum alive and take another step forward. Don't stop.

DAY 119: BE A NEW ARTIST

Choose to see all the ways you can make your dreams a reality. When you were younger, imagining the life you wanted, you didn't have the insights or experiences you possess now. Today, your life is shaped by new circumstances, giving you a clearer understanding of what's possible and what matters most. With this perspective, it's time to embrace the idea of becoming a new kind of artist. This version of you can adapt, explore and create in ways you never imagined before. Your tools and materials might be the same, but your expression – shaped by the people, experiences and growth you've encountered – has evolved. Change isn't the loss of who you are; it's the evolution of your voice and vision.

CHALLENGE

Reflect on how your art or creative process has changed over time. Choose one piece of your past work and reinterpret it today using your current perspective. Notice how your growth influences the way you express yourself now.

DAY 120: SHORT AND SWEET

Hi, this is that clichéd reminder that you've heard 1,000 times and here is 1,001.

It's not too late. You haven't squandered your life. What matters most is that you're here right now. You haven't missed the boat. Today, we choose who we want to be and together, we're going to become that person. That's all there is to it!

CHALLENGE

Write down one thing you've always wanted to do but felt it was 'too late' to start. Now, take one small step towards it today – research, sketch or take action. Prove to yourself that the boat hasn't sailed – you're still on the dock, ready to embark.

DAY 121: REVISION NOT FAIL

Did you forget that you're allowed to revise? With art, you can rewind and revisit in ways you can't in real life. Don't let the idea of starting again overwhelm you. Remember, we never truly start from scratch; we carry the knowledge and experience from our first attempts. So, who cares if the first try wasn't exactly what you envisioned? Revise with passion! Revise with desire! How amazing is it that we have the opportunity to go back and make things better? This is your message to the world – let's ensure it's the very best it can be. Embrace the journey of revision as a powerful step towards creating something truly meaningful. Revising doesn't mean you failed. It means you've gained clarity and are now ready to come back even stronger. So, let's go!

CHALLENGE

Find that one project or idea you set aside and revisit it today. Look at it with fresh eyes and see if new inspiration sparks. Sometimes, what you once passed off just needs a second chance to come to life.

DAY 122: NO GUARANTEES

We will always inspire, always encourage, always push you to keep going. But a guarantee? That's something no one on this planet can offer. You might feel it in your bones – you *know* you're on the right path, and this project is going to be the one to shatter that glass ceiling. But here's the thing: the journey is so much more important than the 'winning' moment.

A long time ago, people decided that trophies were the moment you get to celebrate your work. But in reality, the work, the achievement, the *victory* happens every single day. The glory isn't in the final award, it's in that small studio space, in the 567th brushstroke you took today. It's in showing up, refining and loving what you create.

Winning isn't a single moment, it's the life you're building through every stroke, every note, every step forward. So, keep going, not for the promise of a shiny finish line, but for the love of what you're creating *right now*.

CHALLENGE

Take a moment to document your process – snap a photo of your workspace, record a quick video of yourself creating, or write a note about what you loved (or learned) during today's work. Remind yourself that *this* is the real victory.

DAY 123: ANOTHER 'F' WORD

FEEDBACK is not failure. Read that twice. We know that the word 'feedback' can often rear its head on those tough days when it feels like everything is falling apart. It can catch you off guard during your highest highs and your lowest lows, and it's usually met with the same eye roll. But here's the thing: art is all about perspective, right? We need to shift our mindset and start viewing feedback as just another perspective – an opportunity for growth, not a personal attack.

Embrace it as a tool to refine your craft, to expand your vision and to deepen your understanding of your art. Remember, each piece of feedback is a stepping stone on your creative journey, guiding you towards your next breakthrough. So, the next time feedback comes your way, take a breath, listen and let it inspire you to elevate your work even further. You've got this.

CHALLENGE

Set a timer for 2 minutes and put your personal feelings aside. Reflect honestly on the feedback you've received – how can it elevate your process and help you grow? Focus on the opportunity, not the sting.

DAY 124: INSPIRATION DOESN'T WAIT

Your creativity doesn't wait for the perfect moment. It fashions its own perfect moments out of ordinary ones. The saying 'luck favours the prepared' encapsulates this sentiment perfectly. You want to be primed and ready, like a hunter awaiting the perfect moment to catch creativity as it darts through you from the soles of your feet to your brain. If brilliance were to strike unexpectedly, you'd want to be poised to seize it, wouldn't you? Today, take the initiative to set yourself up for the magic to strike. Prepare yourself for the brilliance waiting to be unleashed. It can only be done through creating.

CHALLENGE

- Prepare: Your creative space is your sanctuary, your haven for inspiration and productivity. It's essential to ensure that whenever you plan to create, your space is primed and ready for you.
- Rest and Recovery: Just like athletes who prioritize rest and recovery to perform at their best, we too must adopt a similar mindset. Physical health directly impacts cognitive function and creative output, so taking care of your body is crucial for sustaining creativity over the long term.

DAY 125: THE CHOICE IS YOURS

There's wanting it, and then there's 'no bullshit' wanting it – going after it with everything you've got. You have to carve out the time and clear out every distraction. Get serious with yourself and your art. You know the difference. You can feel when you're truly chasing your passion versus when you're just fighting to find it. That conflict you feel half the time? It comes from knowing you aren't doing everything necessary to breathe life into what you love. So, what will you do about that? Will you choose you? Choose your art? Or will you keep making excuses?

CHALLENGE

Dive in with everything you've got, as if your passion depends on it. Feel the difference between 'wanting it' and *truly going* after it. The choice is yours – make it count.

DAY 126: STOP WASTING TIME

How many years of your life will you waste feeling insecure and measuring yourself against your creative friends? How many more days will slip by while you hold yourself back? Remember, you don't own every creative idea under the sun. The key is to rework, evolve and focus on your unique journey. When you finally lift your head and look at what others are doing, do it to find inspiration. Let their successes remind you that creativity is possible, that success is attainable, and that dreaming big is not just allowed, but essential. Cheer for others; it's a practice that nurtures your own growth. Teach your subconscious that this is how we thrive – we work hard not only to believe in others but to believe in ourselves.

CHALLENGE

Write down three creative friends or peers whose work you admire. Next to each name, list one specific thing about their work or journey that inspires you.

DAY 127: YOUR WHY

We saw a big sign in the middle of the city yesterday that read: 'Remember why you started.' Maybe it was fun, maybe it was freeing, maybe it made you feel the most alive and like yourself. Anything you do in this life that makes you feel true to who you are in this world is worth every ounce of struggle. When you choose your art, you choose yourself. How beautiful is that?

Whatever emotion you are faced with in this season of your creation, just remember why the hell you even started. If you are trying to make art that changes perspectives, it will be hard; if you are bringing joy into the world, that will be hard. Anything good worth doing in this world will be hard. That is okay. Accept it, remember it and keep creating. The world needs you.

CHALLENGE

Create a 'Why I Started' artefact. Use your medium – whether it's a sketch, a few lines of poetry, a song snippet or even a small sculpture – to capture the essence of why you began your creative journey. Let this piece become a touchstone, something you can revisit whenever the path feels tough, reminding you of the joy and purpose that started it all.

DAY 128: SHOW UP

Just a reminder: showing up doesn't mean being perfect. It doesn't mean having every detail polished or delivering a flawless pitch. It simply means embracing a posture of willingness. You're willing to put in the work, to push past your deepest self-doubt and to do whatever it takes to drive your life forward. That's what showing up truly means. You know the difference! There's a time and place for coasting, but when you're an artist in a make-or-break moment, this isn't one of them. If you are looking for your reason to create today . . . this is it. Do it because you have no other choice and you simply must express yourself.

CHALLENGE

Don't overthink it; let your willingness to express be the win. Celebrate the act of showing up, not the outcome.

DAY 129: HOLD IT LIGHTLY

It's not that deep – yet it is, and isn't, all at once. But let's focus on the lighter side. Life is like a handful of sand: hold it loosely. This doesn't mean you don't care – on the contrary, it's essential to care deeply. The goal is to invest in your art without letting it consume you to the point of despair. Hold your dreams lightly, yet firmly. Be steadfast in your vision, but flexible in your approach to achieving it. See how that balance works? Embrace the journey with open arms, allowing your creativity to flow without the weight of perfection.

CHALLENGE

Create a 'handful of sand' project. Pick an idea you've been holding on to tightly and reinterpret it in a playful, unexpected way.

DAY 130: SUCCESS ISN'T ONE SIZE FITS ALL

So, you're not at the pinnacle of what the world deems 'success'. But consider this: only a tiny fraction of people ever reach those narrow definitions. We're often conditioned to believe that success only counts if it fits a specific mould – whether that's a corner office, a best-seller list or some elite stage. This mindset can derail our passion, making us feel like we've failed ourselves and our dreams. But real success isn't confined to any one destination; it's about finding meaning and purpose in every step of your journey. Your path is yours alone and it's unfolding exactly as it should. You're not off-track – you're exactly where you're meant to be.

CHALLENGE

Redefine success for yourself. Write down three ways your creative journey has brought meaning or fulfilment to your life, regardless of external recognition.

DAY 131: UNPLUG

Mental balance can feel unattainable when you work and live in chaos, leaving you struggling to complete your tasks. Here's a simple suggestion: unplug. Take just 45 minutes away from the noise. The world won't fall apart, we promise. In that brief pause, you'll find the clarity and calm to bring your work full circle. Unplug from your phone, your laptop, this book even. Bye.

CHALLENGE

Unplug.

DAY 132: DARE TO PLAY

Why do you fear losing? Life is a game, and you hold the cards. It's your game, your rules. If something isn't working, don't hesitate to rewrite the script. Turn everything upside down and embrace whatever comes next. Remember, what feels like a loss can be a fresh start in disguise. The only true failure lies in letting fear dictate your actions, preventing you from trying. So, step forward boldly . . . you can't truly lose when you dare to play.

CHALLENGE

What's a new way you can 'play' today? Think beyond the typical idea of fun – play can mean experimenting with a new technique, exploring an unfamiliar medium or reimagining an old idea in a fresh way. Let curiosity guide you and see where it takes you.

DAY 133: KEEPER OF THE KEYS

Express boldly. Express without apology. Express fearlessly. Just express. It doesn't matter how, why or where – what matters is that you do what you were created to do today. You deserve to take up space, to share your voice, to create unapologetically. If you've been convinced otherwise – by someone else or even by yourself – they were wrong. Maybe you feel unworthy, like you've missed your shot or failed somewhere along the way. But life isn't a house with locked doors or closed windows. It's a limitless force, alive with endless opportunities, all waiting for you to activate them. You hold the keys. You always have. It's time to unlock your potential and step into the life that's yours to create.

CHALLENGE

What is a door you are afraid to open? Can you open it today?

DAY 134: CLARITY IS COMING

Failure. Change. Clarity. Pivot. Opportunity. Sometimes, we're thrust into new paths without having chosen them ourselves. How could we, surrounded by billions of people making choices of their own? We are constantly part of the cause and effect of the universe unfolding around us. As creatives, when we feel backed into a corner, it's our moment. This is the time to stand tall, even if the path ahead scares us or wasn't our choice. If this is where you find yourself right now, it's where you are meant to be. Embrace this moment as clarity and recognize your strength. You have no other choice but to move forward.

CHALLENGE

Create space for clarity today. Tidy your workspace, take a walk or simply sit in silence for a few minutes. Clear the noise – physically or mentally – and open yourself up to whatever inspiration is ready to flow in.

DAY 135: STUCK

Stuck brains, stuck paintbrushes, stuck keyboards . . . It can feel like everything is at a standstill, and that physical stagnation only compounds the frustration. But feeling stuck is not an option. Movement is essential to breaking free from this cycle. You have the power to shift your perspective and reignite your creativity. Start by proving to your brain that you are capable of movement and flow. Do something small to shift your state– breathe, stretch or get your body moving. These small actions can create ripples in your creative process, helping you regain momentum.

So, when you feel the weight of discouragement, don't let it hold you down. Move your body. Move your mind. You have the power to navigate through the swamp of doubt and find your way back to the imaginative space you once inhabited.

CHALLENGE

Break the cycle of stuckness with movement. Choose one action – take a 10-minute walk, stretch with intention or do a simple breathing exercise. As you move, think about how this physical shift mirrors the creative flow you're working towards. Let your body lead the way to unsticking your mind.

DAY 136: BE INSPIRED

Who says what you're working on right now needs to be seen, sold or shared with the masses? If you're too focused on the end result, you're missing the beauty of the moment. The spark of inspiration deserves to be savoured. Why are we so quick to jump into execution mode? Today, let yourself just be inspired. Create something for the pure joy of it, something that makes you smile and brings you peace. Remember, this new idea exists because of all the hours you've poured into everything else. So, before you rush into action, take a breath and enjoy this moment when it's all yours – relish that feeling as it fills you from top to bottom.

CHALLENGE

Create something today that you have no intention of sharing or finishing. Let it be just for you – a doodle, a melody, a free write or even a mood board of inspiration. Focus on the joy of the process, not the outcome. Let yourself simply *be inspired*.

DAY 137: REWORK THE WHEEL

Cool, let's try again. Let's keep pushing, searching and embracing the idea of reworking the wheel. You may reach a point in your creative journey where you feel that growth has stalled. If your goal is to be a professional creative and you're content to keep thriving where you are, then by all means, stay put.

However, if you sense that this path isn't fulfilling you anymore, it might be time to explore new horizons. Remember, you have not failed; you are simply evolving. Just like a plant needs a bigger pot to thrive, you owe it to yourself to ensure your environment supports your growth. Embrace this change and create space for the amazing possibilities that await you!

CHALLENGE

Take 10 minutes today to reflect on your creative environment. Ask yourself: is this space – physically, mentally or creatively – allowing me to grow? If not, brainstorm one small change you can make to expand your horizons, whether it's rearranging your workspace, exploring a new medium or setting a fresh goal. Plant yourself in a space where you can thrive.

DAY 138: ART SAVED MY LIFE

Not everything is for gain. Art is not always something that can be sold or shared with others. Art as therapy can heal you in ways you never thought possible. This is your time to try and express the things inside that hold you back. You can't always talk things out. As creatives, we were put on this world to express. In order to heal, we may need to express some things before we can put words to them. So, this is your permission. Let it out so you can move forward. Paint it out, sing it out, move it out . . . whatever you need to do is your movement. You are sensitive and intuitive. Have patience with yourself and heal like a creative would. Express.

CHALLENGE

Choose one emotion or thought you've been holding inside and express it creatively. This isn't for anyone else; it's for you. Let your art help you heal and move forward.

DAY 139: LEGACY

Treat your art with the respect it deserves. What are we really talking about? Your legacy. Consider this: you might be working on something right now that will outlast your time on this Earth. That's the responsibility you carry. It's about feeling the pressure and necessity to fully engage with whatever project you're currently pursuing. Don't just wing it. Don't rest on past achievements. Don't assume you can just get this one done without full commitment. Creating something that has the potential to inspire future generations requires every ounce of your dedication and practice. Remember, your creative legacy is not something you will fully realize in your lifetime – that's the essence of a legacy. So, prepare yourself for that legacy. Believe in it. Will it into existence and invest everything you have. This is the path you're on, and it's an important one. Never forget that.

CHALLENGE

Treat your current project like it's part of your legacy. Take one intentional action today to elevate it – rewrite a section, refine a detail or push beyond 'good enough'. Imagine it as something that could inspire future generations and give it the respect and commitment it deserves.

DAY 140: ALIGNMENT

Alignment is that season when your energy, purpose and creativity click into place. It feels like a warm summer day where endless possibilities stretch out before you. There's a unique energy in the air . . . one of focus, productivity and expansion. For creatives, this is when we feel most alive, challenged and in perfect alignment with our purpose. It's a coveted time that requires deep focus, where everything seems to click into place. Yet, it's also when distractions inevitably emerge, testing our commitment. But when we choose to stay focused, despite life's interruptions, we unlock the true power of this season, allowing our creative work to flourish. Bask in this season. It won't last forever.

CHALLENGE

Protect your season of alignment. Today, identify one distraction that's been pulling your focus away and consciously set it aside. Use the time and energy saved to dive deeply into a project that makes you feel most alive. Bask in this moment of alignment and let your creativity flourish.

DAY 141: CLARITY

You're growing. It's normal not to feel that progress every single day but rest assured, it is happening. You're making the moves to reach the next opportunity. If a door closes in your face, simply say thank you. When you jump off a cliff, you have two options: you can sprout wings and fly or you can hit the ground. Remember, hitting the ground isn't failure; it's clarity. That impact can be sobering, but it gives you the insight you need to strategize your next steps. So, get up, brush yourself off and keep your chin up. The door of clarity has opened for you.

CHALLENGE

Create a 'Door of Clarity' map. On a piece of paper, draw a door and write the setback or closed opportunity on one side. On the other side, write three new opportunities or insights that emerged because of it. Add one action step you'll take to walk through that door today and embrace what's next.

DAY 142: SEE

Open your eyes to the good. Recognize the greatness around you. Find inspiration in the small moments. Cultivate gratitude for what you have. Embrace forgiveness, extend grace and appreciate the beauty in everything – whether it's the extraordinary or the mundane. See the ordinary as a canvas for your creativity. Understand that the everyday moments are filled with potential. To be grounded is to acknowledge the truth of your life and your art.

So, take a moment to truly see. **See.**

CHALLENGE

Start a 'Seeing Journal'. For one day, write or sketch every small detail that catches your eye – a crack in the pavement, a stranger's smile, the way sunlight hits your desk. At the end of the day, reflect on how these moments reveal beauty in the mundane and could inspire your next creative piece.

DAY 143: I DARE YOU

Just jump. Just fly. Just find out if you've got it. But do it through action. The only way you will know if you have what it takes or not is to do the damn thing. We dare you.

CHALLENGE

You know what you have to do.

DAY 144: DATE YOUR ART

Creating art is much like nurturing a relationship – it has its seasons. There are times when your creative process feels passionate and sweet, bursting with inspiration and joy. Other times, it can feel monotonous and boring, dragging on like a long, tedious day. But just like any meaningful relationship, it's work. Day in and day out, you must put your art before everything else because you love it.

So, how much do you truly love your art? How much do you cherish the life you're crafting with each stroke of the brush or keystroke on the page? Are you willing to put it all on the line, to invest your time, energy and heart into it? Your commitment to your art is a reflection of your love for it. Embrace the ups and downs, knowing that every season contributes to the richness of your creative journey. Choose to show up, to engage and to cultivate this relationship.

CHALLENGE

Write a love letter to your art. Reflect on why you fell in love with it, what it gives you and how you've grown together through the seasons.

DAY 145: LET THEM CREATE

Let them create. Embrace the beauty of your creative friends venturing off on their own journeys. Their art unfolds, fresh and fun, without you – just as it should. You may feel a twinge of comparison or doubt but remember: their growth is not a reflection of your worth. It's a reminder that creativity thrives in abundance. Your creative fire will shine even brighter when you let go of comparison and step into your own light. So, let them create. And as they blossom, allow yourself to flourish alongside them. Trust that your time to shine will come, and when it does, you'll bring with you the richness of your experiences and the depth of your creativity.

CHALLENGE

Celebrate a creative friend today. Reach out to someone whose work inspires you – send them a message, share their art or simply tell them you admire what they're doing.

DAY 146: DO YOU

Even when you go out of your way to support others and do right by them, it's natural to prioritize your own needs and aspirations. So, when people make choices that don't include you, remember, it's not personal. Their decisions may impact you personally, but everyone must navigate their creative path, even if it feels selfish at times. In the realm of artistry, we all face moments when we must choose our own direction, even if it means stepping away from what's familiar or comfortable. It's essential to recognize that these choices are often necessary for personal growth and creative evolution.

Your friends, colleagues and fellow creatives are on their own journeys, and while their choices may not involve you, they are striving for their own fulfilment and expression. Allow them that space and give yourself the same freedom. It's okay to be self-focused in your artistic decisions. You have to and that's enough. Be bold.

CHALLENGE

Reflect on a moment when someone's creative choice felt personal to you. Write down how their decision may have helped them grow or evolve. Then, turn inward and identify one bold, self-focused choice you can make for your own creative journey. Take action on it today – no guilt, just growth.

DAY 147: PLAN FOR IT

Start planning for your dreams to take shape. Imagine your ideas coming to life, envision the money flowing into your bank account and picture everything falling into place just as it should. Often, we spend more time anticipating the worst-case scenarios than we do celebrating the possibilities. So, when that money finally drops into your account, what's your plan? When the studio reaches out for your script, is it already written? When you get the opportunity to perform, have you practised and prepared? It's time to shift your mindset: plan for success. Begin living your life in alignment with the person you aspire to be. Visualize your goals and take intentional steps towards them. Posture yourself for the abundance that is rightfully yours. Remember, you have the power to shape your reality. So, plan for it – because it is yours for the taking.

CHALLENGE

Choose one of your big goals and imagine it's already happening. What would you need in place? Write down the steps or tools required, then pick one to act on today. As you complete each item, check it off and remind yourself that you're actively shaping your future, one step at a time.

DAY 148: ARM THE ARTISTS

It's time we embrace a mindset of discipline, preparation and resilience. Just like athletes, we need to fuel our bodies and minds to reach our creative potential. Training, practice and intentional preparation are what allow us to show up on 'game day' and perform at our best. Think about it: we are what we eat, who we surround ourselves with and the stories we tell ourselves. Nourish your body with the right fuel. Engage with people who inspire and challenge you. Develop a positive and empowering inner dialogue. We're the athletes of perspective, shaping the world through our unique visions and creative abilities. Let's own that identity, train with purpose and step boldly into our arenas. The time is now. Let's be ready to play.

CHALLENGE

Write a short, empowering mantra that affirms your identity as a creative athlete, e.g. 'I am focused, prepared and unstoppable.' Repeat it to yourself before you start your next creative session.

DAY 149: GET SPECIFIC

As creatives, it's time to get specific about achieving our next goals. Whatever you're working on – whether it's finishing a project, building a portfolio or starting something entirely new – clarity is key. Success doesn't just happen; it's built with intention and focus. Ask yourself: what does success look like? How can you break it down into manageable, actionable steps? Maybe it's committing to a daily practice or hitting a set milestone each week. Until you set a clear target, you won't fully understand what you're working towards. Get clear on your vision. Get serious about your commitments. Dive deep into your creative process and start becoming the artist you've always dreamed of being. When you embrace specificity, you transform dreams into achievable milestones.

CHALLENGE

Write down your ultimate creative vision – the artist you dream of becoming. Then, break it into three specific milestones you can work towards. Choose one milestone and outline a single step you'll take today to move closer to it. Clarity turns dreams into action – start now.

DAY 150: STOP GASLIGHTING YOURSELF

Gaslighting yourself is a dangerous trap. When you dismiss your feelings, telling yourself they aren't valid, you undermine your own emotional truth. Remember, vulnerability and creativity are deeply personal endeavours. When you put your heart into your art, it's an expression of who you are. So, if you find yourself feeling hurt by feedback or betrayed by a collaborator or fellow creative – breathe. It's okay to feel that sting. Acknowledge that it is personal because it is. Your feelings are valid and your reactions are natural. Embrace the pain as part of the process; it signifies your passion and dedication to your craft. We will rebuild from this. Trust in your ability to create anew, knowing that this experience can fuel your growth. Your art is yours, and you have the power to shape it in ways that reflect your true self.

CHALLENGE

Create a 'Validation Vault'. Write down one instance where your feelings about your art were dismissed, whether by others or by yourself. Then, on the same page, write a response validating your emotions and reclaiming your truth, e.g. 'It hurt because I care deeply and that's a strength, not a weakness.' Let this practice remind you to honour your creative journey and use these moments to fuel your growth.

DAY 151: PROTECT YOUR ENERGY

You've been helping a friend creatively, putting in those reps, and it feels good – at first. There's gratitude, excitement and that warm glow of collaboration. But then, as time goes on, you start to feel the weight of expectations settle in. The magic you were once so happy to share now feels like an obligation. You may have hit your wall. It's essential to recognize when that shift happens. Your creativity is a precious resource, and it deserves respect and acknowledgement. Protect your energy and passion. Step back, reassess your involvement and remember: your creativity should never be taken for granted. You have the power to choose how and where you direct your gifts, so make sure it's in spaces that nourish your soul, not deplete it.

CHALLENGE

Reflect on your current collaborations or creative commitments. Ask yourself: *Does this still energize me or has it become an obligation?* Write down one boundary you can set to protect your creative energy – whether it's saying no to new requests, limiting your time or stepping back entirely.

DAY 152: WATCH OUT

There's an old children's song that goes, 'Oh, be careful little eyes what you see. Oh, be careful little ears what you hear.' For creatives, those words should resonate deeply. We must be vigilant guardians of our minds, ensuring our creativity remains as pure and untainted as possible. Negativity has no place in our creative spaces. It's all too easy to fall into the trap of gossiping about other artists who are bravely putting themselves out there. But remember, each creative journey is unique, and tearing others down only clouds your own channel of inspiration. What you want to create needs to come from within you, untouched by the murky waters of judgement and envy. Keep your mind clear and nurture the seeds of your imagination with positivity and support. Surround yourself with encouragement and focus on your own artistic growth.

CHALLENGE

Be a guardian of your creative space today. Identify one source of negativity – whether it's gossip, self-doubt or judgement – and consciously replace it with something uplifting. Compliment another artist, immerse yourself in inspiring work or journal about your creative goals. Clear the noise and make room for positivity to fuel your imagination.

DAY 153: MOVING TARGETS

We're all doing everything we can to make it work. The truth is: the target keeps moving – and it always will. The win is coming, but sometimes you have to hold your breath a little longer. You don't do this because it's easy or because anyone's cheering you on. You do it because you can't imagine doing anything else. So, keep creating. Even when it feels like you're out of breath, keep going. Every attempt sharpens your skills, refines your vision and brings you closer. Every near miss is progress in disguise. And when you finally hit that bullseye, you'll realize every miss, stumble and moment of doubt was worth it. The journey is what makes the win so powerful. Keep aiming. It's coming.

CHALLENGE

Write down three times you came close to achieving something but didn't quite hit the mark. Next to each, note what you learned or how it helped you grow. Use this reflection as fuel to aim again today – take one step towards your next shot, knowing each attempt sharpens your path to success.

DAY 154: YOU CAN BE FREE

Today, set yourself free. There's a truth inside you that needs to be spoken, a weight that needs to be lifted. When you finally face the worst possible outcome, you'll gain clarity – no matter how it turns out. And if the worst thing is that the world blows up, well, at that point, it won't even matter! You'll realize it wasn't as terrifying as you imagined – and that's when you'll feel truly free. You hold the key to your own freedom. In your creativity, if you aren't brutally honest with yourself, your art has no space to breathe. Yes, beautiful art can come from holding back and people-pleasing, but only for so long. Today, try out honesty. Confront the parts of honesty that scare you. Create from that place and see what happens.

CHALLENGE

Create from your raw, unfiltered truth today. Write, draw or express the thing you've been too afraid to confront – the fear, the desire, the hope or the pain. Let go of perfection and people-pleasing and allow your honesty to take shape. What does freedom look like in your art?

DAY 155: COMMISERATE SOMETIMES

There's a special beauty in commiserating with other creatives. Sometimes, it's okay to let your guard down and be raw about where you are in the process – what's pissing you off, what's not working. There's power in that honesty. We're all in this together, trying to make something out of nothing, facing the same setbacks and frustrations. When you open up, you might find someone who's been where you are, who has a solution you hadn't thought of or a fresh perspective to offer. Sharing your struggles is not a sign of weakness; it's a part of the process. Creativity can feel isolating but remember that your fellow creatives understand. So, take a breath, let the walls come down and trust that you're not alone in the chaos. Sometimes, the best breakthroughs happen when we're honest about our struggles.

CHALLENGE

Host a 'Creative Gratitude' moment. Take a few minutes to write down three things you admire about the work of artists you know or follow. Share one of these with them directly or post it publicly. Celebrate their creativity and watch how it inspires positive energy in your own work.

DAY 156: MIRRORS OF EACH OTHER

We carry worlds within us, shifting between doubt and confidence, inspiration and exhaustion, all in a matter of moments. The beauty of it is that no matter how unique we each feel, we're also mirrors of one another. Every creative soul reflects pieces of another. The insecurities, the dreams, the highs of inspiration, the lows of feeling lost – these are universal among us. What you see in yourself, you can often find in others, and what you create may resonate with someone else in a way you never imagined. We're connected through this shared experience, like a series of mirrors reflecting light back and forth.

CHALLENGE

Choose one feeling you've had recently – doubt, joy or inspiration – and express it through your art in a way that could resonate with others. Whether it's a sketch, poem or song, let your creation reflect the shared experience of being a creative soul. Share it if you feel inspired, and let it become a connection point.

DAY 157: BE THE LIGHT

When one of us shines, it lights the way for others. When one of us falls into darkness, it's a familiar struggle that others recognize. We're all navigating this creative path together, and seeing each other helps us see ourselves more clearly. The beauty of creativity is in this exchange – how we inspire and are inspired, reflecting the journey of every other artist we meet. We have a sacred community, and we should share love with it. Social media often tries to compare us, to pit us against each other, but we have the power to rewrite that narrative – it can be a place of inspiration and love, somewhere to uplift one another and celebrate each other's wins. There's space for all of us to shine, and when we do, it's a light that reaches far beyond ourselves. Let's choose to be that light for each other.

CHALLENGE

Be the light today. Share the work of another artist you admire on social media or in conversation and write a few words about how they inspire you. Let your platform – no matter how small or large – be a space to uplift, celebrate and reflect the collective light of our creative community.

DAY 158: DEFENSIVENESS

Being defensive is not the same as protecting your art. You can stand by your vision with respect while still allowing space for feedback and collaboration. Creativity thrives in openness, curiosity and a willingness to see beyond our own vision. Instead of getting defensive, listen. Take in what's being said. Understand that feedback is not an attack; it's an opportunity. Every piece of feedback, whether it resonates or not, holds a chance to expand your view, refine your craft and grow. Let go of the ego.

CHALLENGE

The next time you receive feedback, pause before reacting. Write down what's being said without judgement. Then, ask yourself: *What can I learn from this?* Even if it's not what you wanted to hear, look for one takeaway you can use to refine your work. Embrace feedback as a tool for growth, not a challenge to your vision.

DAY 159: BUY IN

Today, no matter what your creative role is – big or small – ask yourself: how can you buy in and truly show up? Whether you're the director of the movie or the intern making popcorn, show up completely and with gratitude. The world may not always deserve your dedication, your willingness to give your all, but **you** do. Do it for yourself. Be the best at whatever hat you have to wear today, and when you rest your head tonight, remember that you earned it. You showed up. You did the damn thing. And that is more than enough.

CHALLENGE

Fully 'buy in' to your creative vision today. Commit to one idea or project you've been hesitant about and take a decisive action to move it forward. Show yourself that you're all in, and watch how your commitment fuels momentum.

DAY 160: IT'S ALL HARD

The hardest part of this process is something you can't fully predict –
it's the relentless grind of showing up every single day and doing the
thing you said you were going to do. It's the endless calls, the constant
connecting of people, dots and projects. No one else will care at the
level you do because this is your creative baby. Day after day, you'll
find yourself being the ringleader, pushing forward when no one else
will. You will get tired, and you will hear 'no' more times than you
can count. But you will keep creating. You will keep repeating. And
in that persistence, you will find yourself and discover what you're
truly made of.

CHALLENGE

Commit to one action today that moves your project forward, no
matter how small. Whether it's making a call, sending an email or
organizing one part of your creative process, show up for your vision.
The grind is made up of these small, consistent steps.

DAY 161: WARRIOR

By the end of this journey, you will be a different kind of creative. You will be more thoughtful, seeing the world with new eyes. You will be someone willing and ready to put in the work, day in and day out, because that's what it takes. Your craft demands your attention every single day, and not a day should go by without nurturing it.

Yes, you are shedding old layers, but you are also building up your artist armour. You are becoming a warrior, and that's no easy feat. It takes courage, resilience and an unwavering commitment to the work you love. Every layer that falls is replaced by strength and determination, shaping you into a creative who's ready to face whatever comes.

CHALLENGE

Imagine you're designing your own creative armour. Today, identify one limiting belief or habit that holds you back and transform it into something empowering. For example, if you often feel 'stuck', reframe it as 'a space for new ideas to emerge'. Act on this new belief by taking one brave, small step in your work today – something that pushes you forward and reinforces your strength.

DAY 162: THE EVIDENCE WILL CATCH UP

What if the only thing standing between you and the life you want is time? Not talent, not luck – just time. The work you're doing now might not have results yet, but that doesn't mean it's not working. Growth is often invisible until it isn't.

Every idea, every project, every action you take is a seed. You may not see what it's becoming, but something is happening beneath the surface. Don't let the lack of immediate proof convince you to stop. Stay consistent. Stay close to the vision. The evidence will catch up.

CHALLENGE

Write a short note to your future self, the one who's seeing results. Remind them what it felt like to keep going without evidence. Then take one action today that future you will thank you for.

DAY 163: EXPAND

You are being called to expand your capacity – to stretch yourself beyond what you thought you could handle, to do the things you know you must do in this life. This isn't about working on a schedule or following a set timeline; it's about diving deep into the work, losing yourself in it and emerging on the other side changed. Here's how it works: once you expand, even if it's uncomfortable, you stay there. You don't shrink back to playing it small or retreat to your old limits. You make a home in your new expansiveness and learn to thrive there. Your creative work needs that kind of expansiveness. It needs your hungry energy to flourish, your willingness to go beyond what's easy or predictable. So, keep expanding, keep pushing your boundaries and grow into every inch of that new space.

CHALLENGE

You can do more than you think. Where in your work today can you expand your capacity?

DAY 164: GROW

You have to make it to the other side of the growing pains this time. You cannot give up. You cannot back down. Do not mistake difficulty and discomfort for signs that it's not meant to be. This is meant to be. You are meant to be. And what you are breathing life into is meant to be. This journey should feel like that deep, aching pull that reaches beyond your bones, past the soles of your feet. It's the kind of hard that you feel in your entire being – but it's worth it.

Remember when you were a kid, and your legs cramped from growing? There were no takebacks then; growth was inevitable. You had to grow, and you had to become. This is that season right now. You are becoming. So, take a deep breath. Embrace the growing pains. Don't be afraid to step into what's waiting for you on the other side.

CHALLENGE

What is one area of your life right now where you're feeling the growing pains? Reflect on where you feel stretched, challenged or even unsure. That's the space where growth is happening. How can this infuse into your creative process?

DAY 165: IT LOOKS DIFFERENT

Embrace the fact that this process doesn't look anything like you thought it would. Look at your hands – these hands that create, that keep showing up every day – and be thankful for them, however they may look. Appreciate the spaces that have held you through this journey, however imperfect they are. And most of all, be grateful you're not exactly where you want to be yet, because that's why you keep going. Wherever you are on this swing of ups and downs, remember that growth and newness are things we all crave. It might look nothing like what you pictured, but the fact that you're searching, seeing and seeking – this is what shapes your reality. Make this journey your own, imperfections and all. One day, looking back, these hard moments will be memories you cherish. You won't believe what came from this season.

CHALLENGE

Reframe it: Instead of focusing on what didn't happen, ask yourself:
- What did I learn from this?
- How can I use what I've created in a new way?
- What unexpected opportunities could come from this?

Commit to one step today to embrace the unexpected. Maybe it's adapting your vision, starting over with fresh inspiration or letting the work lead you somewhere new.

DAY 166: MONEY IS A BY-PRODUCT

Yes, you need money. But it can't be everything to you. There are times when we all take on projects for the paycheque, and there's no shame in that. But that is not what this journey is about, and it's not why you picked up this book. We are here for your soul. We are here to create the kind of art that feels like once-in-a-lifetime magic – something all-consuming, something that leaves a mark. Money isn't the enemy; it's a tool. It's something you absolutely need to bring your visions to life, to support your craft and to keep building. But the truth is, money is a by-product of doing the work that matters. It's not the reason you do it; it's what comes when you're living in your purpose, creating art that makes people feel something. It will come, but it can't be your North Star.

CHALLENGE

Think about a project you'd create if money wasn't a factor, something that lights up your soul. Take one small step towards it today, even if it's just writing the idea down or dreaming about what it could be.

DAY 167: IT'S OK TO CHILL

Today, we give you permission to rest. You've been grinding, morning, noon and night. Life is buzzing and your art is demanding, but today, let this be a reminder that your creativity flourishes when you allow yourself to rest. You are still a creative if you choose to pause. Rest your body, rest your eyes and rest your mind. Give yourself the gift of stillness. Your art will be better because of it – renewed, refreshed and filled with the gratitude that only comes from honouring yourself. Today, rest. Tomorrow, create from a place of renewal.

CHALLENGE

Take a moment to rest – step away from your work and find stillness, even if just for 5 minutes. Let this be the pause that renews your creativity for tomorrow.

DAY 168: YOUR YOUNGER SELF

Create for your younger self – the one who dreamed big but didn't yet know how to make it happen. But maybe it's not just about you. Maybe it's about creating for the younger version of yourself out there right now.

Make something that sparks curiosity, that ignites the imagination of someone who feels just like you once did. Create for those who need a sign, a mentor or a guiding hand to show them what's possible.

It's bigger than just you. It's about all the dreamers out there, waiting for a sign that they can do it too. They need you. Your story matters to them more than you realize. Create for them and in doing so, you might set something extraordinary into motion.

CHALLENGE

Create something today that would have inspired your younger self or someone just like them. If you can't think of anything, go back to a film or something that inspired you as a kid.

DAY 169: RIPPLE EFFECT

Think about all the tiny, intricate moments that happen each day because every person is making their own choices. Your choices matter. In Japanese culture, there is a deep sense of community – a belief that individual actions contribute to the greater good, that it's truly all for one and one for all. You see this reflected in the cleanliness of their public spaces, the sense of order and the collective respect for rules. Imagine if creatives approached their work and each other with a similar mindset. If we each saw our art not just as an individual pursuit but as part of a larger creative community, what kind of ripple effect could we create? What if we made choices that lifted each other up, inspired each other and kept the creative world thriving for everyone? The potential is limitless. One small act of support, one choice to create with intention, could spark a movement that resonates far beyond what we could imagine – ripples turning into waves of change, inspiration and connection.

CHALLENGE

Take 10 minutes to write down one small action or choice you made today. Imagine how that action might ripple out to impact others – directly or indirectly – whether it's showing kindness, sharing your work or simply being present.

DAY 170: LET YOUR ART REEK OF YOU

Whatever you share, make, post, create or breathe into existence – let it carry the unmistakable imprint of you. Own yourself, love yourself and let every piece you put out be saturated with your unique style and vision. The only thing no one else on this planet can replicate is your DNA. You're 1 of 1. Embrace that, let it shine through your work and be unapologetically, unmistakably you.

CHALLENGE

Create something today that feels deeply personal – whether it's a piece of art, writing or even a social post. Focus on infusing it with your unique voice, perspective and quirks. When it's done, reflect on how it represents who you are and what makes your creative DNA truly one of a kind.

DAY 171: BOUNDARIES

Let's not confuse apathy for our craft with the feeling of boundaries being crossed. It's easy to keep saying yes, to let others take up all your time and mental real estate. But listen to what your mind and body are telling you. When your brain starts going into protect mode, when it feels like it's being stretched too thin, it's not because you've lost your passion – it's because your boundaries are being tested. Setting limits doesn't mean you care less about your work or the people around you. It means you care enough about your craft, your well-being and your creativity to protect them. Your creativity needs space to breathe, and sometimes that means saying no. Respect your boundaries, and trust that doing so will help you create from a place of strength rather than exhaustion.

CHALLENGE

Take a moment to identify one area in your life where you feel your boundaries are being crossed. Write down one clear, specific action you can take today to protect that space and honour your needs.

DAY 172: TIME IS FOR YOU

The timing of most things in life will rarely align with our desires. What you wanted 10 years ago is different now, shaped by the passage of time. Time is a relentless teacher. It grows us, stretches our beliefs and pushes the boundaries of what we think is possible. 'Only time will tell,' they say. So, what has time taught you? What lessons have emerged from the moments you thought would define you? Consider how time influences your art. You will only grow stronger with time as you remain true to the person you aspire to be in this world. Time is working for you and not against you. It grants us wisdom, and as the days pass, we become more confident in our choices. This wisdom is a key that unlocks our potential.

CHALLENGE

Pause and consider how time influences your creative process. Decide today whether you'll embrace patience, set a timeline or allow the work to unfold naturally.

DAY 173: JUST BE

Who you are today in your space is free of expectation. Allow yourself to exist in this moment without the weight of judgement or the pressure to produce. Embrace the beauty of simply being. This is your time to explore, to play and to create without the confines of what others think you should achieve.

CHALLENGE

Let yourself explore, play or simply sit in stillness – free from judgement or the need to produce. What will come from this approach?

DAY 174: BOUNCE BACK

So, you got a little behind – it's okay. Today, you're back with a fresh perspective and feeling rested. Not every day can be about hitting the grind button and pushing through exhaustion. But today, with the rest you took, you're ready to create more meaningful, lasting work. That's the real goal. Remember, progress isn't always about relentless hustle – sometimes it's about allowing yourself to recharge so you can come back stronger. Today is your day to make it count.

CHALLENGE

Start with one small, meaningful action that gets you back on track – something you've been excited to create or finish. Let today's energy remind you that rest fuels progress, and focus on making this step count.

DAY 175: RELEASE IT

Release your work with power and pride. This is your moment – it's not about how it's received or who shows up to cheer you on. It's about honouring the journey you've taken to bring your vision to life. You've nurtured this creation, poured your time, energy and passion into it. Now, let it stand on its own, knowing you've given it everything you had. Release it, not for validation, but for the simple and profound joy of creating. This is your moment – embrace it fully.

CHALLENGE

Press send, press post or share your work today with full confidence. Celebrate what you've created – it deserves to be seen and you deserve to be proud.

DAY 176: SLOW MOTION

Slow motion is better than no motion. Let that sink in. Progress, no matter how small, is progress. The creative process will never be exactly what you envisioned, and that's okay. It will evolve in ways you didn't anticipate and that unpredictability is what makes it beautiful. Many people give up, not because their art wasn't good, but because it didn't align with their expectations. They let the discrepancy between the vision and reality discourage them. Don't let that be you. Embrace the slow, steady journey, knowing that motion, no matter the pace, is still moving you toward your dreams. Trust in the process, even if it unfolds differently than planned.

CHALLENGE

Make something today – a doodle, a phrase or a few notes of a song – that reflects where you are right now. Let it be a quiet celebration of progress, no matter how small.

DAY 177: START OVER

Starting over isn't quitting, it's evolving. There's a difference. If you once dreamed of being a writer, a designer, a filmmaker or something else entirely, but have fallen out of love with it, that's fine! Ask yourself: what was it about that creative pursuit that you loved? Was it the thrill of bringing ideas to life, building new worlds or the feeling of being seen and appreciated? There's power in the pivot. It's not about giving up; it's about rediscovering what excites you and finding a new way to chase it.

CHALLENGE

Rediscover your spark. Reflect on a creative pursuit you once loved – what thrilled you about it? Today, find one small way to reconnect with that feeling or pivot towards a new path that reignites your excitement.

DAY 178: PURITY IN ART

The only true failure is giving up, stopping altogether. Why? Do you remember why you started? Was this your escape from a small town, a chance to dream bigger? Were you the kid in high heels, putting on shows with your cousins in the living room? That pure, fearless creativity was your essence. So why have you lost touch with it? Has trauma crept in, convincing you that self-expression is too painful? Let's heal that wound. Let's reconnect with the core feeling – that art is freedom. Art gives us the words we cannot speak. Art heals and art saves lives. Don't let fear silence you. Keep creating because this is your voice, your liberation, your purpose.

CHALLENGE

How can we connect back to the freedom in art? Create something today with no rules, no expectations and no plan – just for the pure joy of making. Let yourself play, explore and feel the freedom that comes from creating without constraints.

DAY 179: PLAYING IT SAFE
WON'T SAVE YOU

Playing it safe won't save you. We used to think that being small meant being safe, that staying silent would protect us, that closing our eyes would shield us from what we didn't want to see. On the surface, those ideas seem true, but they don't feel true. Shrinking yourself doesn't keep you from harm – it keeps you from living fully. Playing it safe means missing out on the depth of your own creativity and the powerful impact you could have. Real safety comes from embracing who you are, from stepping into your truth and from creating boldly. Don't let the illusion of safety hold you back – take risks, be seen and trust in the power of your art.

CHALLENGE

We dare you. Be dangerous today – dangerous with your art. Push past your usual vibe and see what wild, unexpected magic you can make.

DAY 180: EMBRACE THE LIGHT

You want to do something meaningful? You want to release positive messages out into the world? Remember, everything comes at a cost – nothing is free. For every good thing you put out, there may be six negative responses. It's the balance of nature – light and dark, forever in conflict. You have to push past the negativity that inevitably comes with doing positive work. You can't let it consume you or control your emotions. You have to keep building, keep growing. When you're growing light, you'll face resistance from the darkness. But that's the journey. Embrace it, rise above it and keep your focus on the light you're bringing to the world.

CHALLENGE

Can you push past the darkness today? Can you lean into the hard stuff and create anyway? Let the shadows guide you to something raw, real and uniquely yours.

DAY 181: SEASONS OF CONNECTION

The people in your life come and go, like the changing seasons. That's not something to mourn – it's part of the beauty of the creative journey. It's a reminder that nothing is permanent, that life flows in cycles, and as we grow and evolve, so do the people who walk alongside us.

Those who align with your creative vision today may not always be there, and that's okay. For now, look around at the ones who inspire you, who share your space and contribute to your art. Be deeply grateful for their presence.

Understand that not everyone will stay, and not everyone is meant to ignite your spark forever. Life is about cherishing the collaborators of this moment while remaining open to new muses and fresh inspiration when it's time to let go. Embrace the ebb and flow.

CHALLENGE

Create from the ebb and flow. Honour the love and lessons from those who have come and gone in your life. Channel the joy and pain into something meaningful today – no relationship is ever a waste. Can you infuse that into what you make?

DAY 182: CREATE WHAT YOU WISH EXISTED

Creating the things you wish existed is what makes art deeply personal. You're tapping into desires buried within your soul, revealing everything you are and everything you aspire to be for the world to see. It takes courage – the kind of cliff-jumping moment where you shout, 'Hey, I exist!' You can only linger in that incubation stage for so long. Every butterfly eventually faces the moment when it must break free. The idea of flying can seem impossible. But remember: it doesn't matter how daunting it feels. 'Seeming impossible' and 'being impossible' are two entirely different realities. Embrace the leap; your soul is waiting on the other side. The beauty of your art lies in its ability to transform the impossible into something breathtaking.

CHALLENGE

What's that one thing you've been holding back, keeping safe in its cocoon? Crack it open today – start, share or set it free, and let the world see what's been waiting to take flight.

DAY 183: STOP RESISTING

The push you're resisting is what will ultimately set you free. But what does that truly mean? Is it the notion that on the other side of a broken vase lies the possibility of a rebuild? Does it mean facing the reality that sometimes things must be discarded, like a piece of art that no longer serves you? Or is it simply acknowledging that as human beings, we are in a constant state of healing and evolution? Consider this: art is an ongoing journey and what lies beyond our ego is an opportunity for profound discovery. Is it better to stumble and learn rather than cling to a fixed idea of perfection? Perhaps, yes. Embracing the messiness of the creative process often leads to unexpected breakthroughs. So, let go of what you thought you knew. Allow yourself to be pushed into the unknown. In that space of uncertainty, you'll find the freedom you so desperately seek.

CHALLENGE

Step out of your own head and go find art in the world today. Let something unexpected inspire you – a mural, a song or even the way light dances through a window.

DAY 184: TOMORROW REMEMBERS TODAY

Have you ever heard it said that tomorrow remembers today? It's a deep truth. Tomorrow isn't shaped by your dreams or aspirations; it's constructed by the actions you take today. Each step you make, every choice you make, lays the foundation for what's to come. Every moment you push through, every idea you breathe life into, is a thread woven into the fabric of your future. So, keep going. Embrace the process, even when it feels daunting. Remember that tomorrow is already looking back, holding space for the choices you make right now. Your present efforts will echo in the days to come, and it's those choices that will create the life you envision. Let tomorrow remember the courage you showed today.

CHALLENGE

Imagine the person you'll be tomorrow – how can you make them proud today? Take one step that sets your future self up for creative success and inspiration.

DAY 185: HOLD THE FLAME

Hold your flame close, no matter how small the glow may seem. Nurture it with care and intention, for your soul needs this light more than you realize. In ancient times, fire was a source of warmth, safety and sustenance. It brought people together, lit the darkness and fuelled the creative spirit. Just as they tended to their fires, we, too, must nurture our inner flames. As a creative in today's world, your spark is your unique vision and voice. It may flicker in the face of doubt, overshadowed by the chaos around you, but it holds the power to ignite inspiration and change. Each moment you dedicate to cultivating your passion, no matter how small, adds to the brightness of your flame. Remember that even the tiniest spark can light up a room, and in a world that often feels dim, your steady glow is needed.

CHALLENGE

What fuels your creative fire? Feed it today – whether it's revisiting a passion, finding inspiration or simply showing up for the work that lights you up.

DAY 186: YOU AND YOU ALONE

Do not dilute your voice to fit someone else's expectations. At the end of the day, and even during it, you are the only person you have. When you look in the mirror, it's you staring back. When you hit the pillow at night, it's you alone with your thoughts. You. How you perceive yourself and how you honour your truth matters more than you realize. Your voice is a reflection of your experiences, your passions and your essence. It's the unique melody that only you can create and silencing it to please others will only dim your light. Authenticity breeds connection, and when you honour your true self, it shows up in the work you share with the world. You owe it to yourself to be your best advocate because when you do, your creativity will flourish.

CHALLENGE

Identify one lie in your head that's holding you back from creating. Replace it with a truth and let that truth guide your process today.

DAY 187: FEAR FADES WITH ACTION

Fear fades with action. The more you step into the arena, the less intimidating it becomes. Every small step you take is like chipping away at a massive boulder that seems insurmountable. You have to face the giant head-on. When you finally force yourself to take that leap – whether it's stepping onto an open mic stage or showcasing your work – you begin to realize how low the stakes truly are. People want to support you; they want to see you shine. They're rooting for your success, not waiting for you to fail. In those moments of vulnerability, you discover a community ready to uplift you, transforming fear into encouragement. Embrace the opportunities that challenge you to grow. Each experience – no matter how daunting – adds to your confidence and resilience.

CHALLENGE

Pick one thing that feels like a giant in your creative life. Take a brave first swing today – no matter how small – and prove to yourself that the stakes aren't as high as they seem.

DAY 188: KID YOU NEEDS YOU

As kids, we all faced that moment of being made fun of for something others deemed weird. It stings, and many of us have carried that pain into our adult lives, allowing those memories to shape our identities. But here's the truth: that 'weird' thing is often what makes you truly cool. Your child brain couldn't conceive of this then, but now is the time to embrace it. Let your freak flag fly in the most artistic sense! It's that unique spark – the quirks, the passions, the eccentricities – that define who you are and fuel your creativity. Those aspects that you once tried to hide are the very things that set you apart. It's time to step into your uniqueness, to share your art unapologetically, and to show the world that embracing the unconventional is not just cool – it's essential. Your authenticity is what holds you together. Don't just be normal – stand out, and let your true self be represented.

CHALLENGE

Think back to a time when you felt lost or unsure as a kid. Create something today that would have inspired or comforted that version of you.

DAY 189: ASPIRATION VS INSPIRATION

Aspiration seeks approval, while inspiration seeks expression. Can you see the difference? This distinction is crucial in how we hold ourselves to a standard. Sometimes, we get so caught up in the desire for validation that we forget the pure joy of creation. Maybe the art isn't the problem right now – maybe it's you. Perhaps you've been stuck in a rut, viewing your creative work through a narrow lens, forgetting the passion that sparked your journey in the first place.

It's time to check in with yourself before you wreck yourself. Reconnect with the heart of what you love and remember why you started creating in the first place. Allow that genuine passion to guide you once again, shifting your focus from seeking external approval to embracing the freedom of expression. When you prioritize inspiration over aspiration, you'll find that the art flows more freely and joyfully, rekindling the spark that drives you. So, step back, breathe and rediscover.

CHALLENGE

Take a moment to reflect: are you creating for approval or for the joy of expression? Focus today on making something purely to inspire and express yourself – free from the need for validation.

DAY 190: GREATNESS COMES FROM ANYWHERE

Let this be a reminder: greatness is not reserved for the select few. It's a state of being available to anyone willing to embrace their journey, learn from their experiences and pour their heart into their work. Greatness can come from anywhere. It doesn't matter where you started or the circumstances you faced along the way. The world is full of stories of those who rose from humble beginnings, who turned challenges into opportunities and who transformed their passions into impactful legacies. Every artist, every creator, every visionary began somewhere – often in places that seemed ordinary or overlooked. It's the drive to pursue your craft, the willingness to take risks and the commitment to keep creating that elevate you from the ordinary to the extraordinary.

CHALLENGE

Greatness is waiting in the work you do with heart. Today, create something that feels like it carries a piece of your soul – let it remind you that greatness is simply showing up as your truest self.

DAY 191: THE MAGIC OF UNEXPECTED DESTINATIONS

Every time you choose to show up for yourself, you're creating a path, even if it feels unclear at times. You may not recognize the opportunities when they come, but the warmth and comfort of those moments will resonate deeply within you. It's in those unexpected encounters that you often find the most profound sense of belonging. So, keep pushing forward, even when the destination feels vague. Trust that every small act of dedication will converge into something beautiful. Your journey may lead you to places that feel like home, even when you weren't consciously seeking them. Embrace the magic of possibility and remember that sometimes the best parts of your life unfold when you least expect them.

CHALLENGE

Let go of second-guessing and trust your instincts today. Create from that place of certainty – if it feels right, it is right.

DAY 192: REGRET

Emotions. Bet you didn't expect to encounter regret. That moment of realization – 'What have I gotten myself into?' – can hit like a wave, leaving you with a throbbing headache and a heavy heart. It's an unpredictable feeling, one that creeps in when you least expect it, often catching you off guard. But here's the truth: you need to feel it sometimes. Regret isn't just a burden; it's a teacher. It urges you to pause, to take a step back from the chaos of creation. It's that gentle nudge that says, 'Hey, maybe you need a break.' So go ahead, close your laptop and head downstairs to make a sandwich. In those moments of stillness, you allow space for reflection. A simple act of nourishing yourself can spark clarity, transforming regret into insight. Remember, every emotion you encounter is part of your journey as a creative. Embrace it, learn from it and let it guide you towards the next steps in your craft. The messy moments often pave the way for the most beautiful breakthroughs.

CHALLENGE

Reflect on one regret that lingers in your creative journey. Instead of letting it weigh you down, let it teach you something valuable – and channel that lesson into what you create today.

DAY 193: LET GO

Letting go can be a bittersweet experience, especially when you watch your art phase out like a fading sunset. But within that melancholy lies a powerful truth: you've mastered a way of creating that has brought you joy and growth. Recognizing when it's time to move on is a sign of maturity in your craft. It's about understanding that the beauty of creation lies not in clinging to the past but in embracing the evolution of your artistry. Each version of your work, each chapter of your creative journey, has led you to this moment. As you release the familiar, you open yourself up to the possibilities of what's next. This transition can feel daunting, but it's also an invitation to innovate and explore new avenues. Embrace the discomfort of letting go; it signifies growth and the promise of new beginnings. You are not losing what you created; you are making space for the next version of yourself to emerge. Trust that each ending brings with it new beginnings. Let that inspire your journey forward.

CHALLENGE

Identify one thing – an idea, project or habit – you've been holding onto that no longer serves you. Embrace the discomfort of releasing it and make space for something new to take root.

DAY 194: STAND ON BUSINESS

It's time to stand on business and truly back yourself. No more playing small or dimming your light; it's time to embody the creative powerhouse you know you are. This is your moment to claim your space and take charge of your narrative. The struggle is real and while you don't need to diminish it, you can harness it as fuel for your fire. Remember, the path may not always be smooth, but that's what makes your journey authentic. Stand tall and own your experiences, for they are the building blocks of your success. You are not just a dreamer; you are a doer. So, rise up, trust your instincts and propel yourself forward with unwavering confidence. Stand on business.

CHALLENGE

Take a deep breath and identify one disappointment weighing on you – whether it's in yourself or someone else. Let it go today, freeing your mind and heart to focus on what's possible instead.

DAY 195: BE YOU

Embrace the gift of being fully yourself. Each inhale is an invitation to explore the depths of your experiences, while each exhale becomes an expression of your unique voice. Your art should reflect not just what you create but who you are at your core. It's not about perfection; it's about authenticity. The beauty of your work lies in its truthfulness – acknowledging the messiness, the joy and the complexities of your journey. Stand tall in your individuality and know that you have the power to inspire others by simply being yourself.

CHALLENGE

Embrace every part of who you are – the good, the messy, the beautiful. Create something today that reflects your authentic self, without worrying what anyone else might think.

DAY 196: DON'T GIVE IN

Don't let negativity claim you – refuse to let cynicism creep in and dim your light. When you lose your light, the darkness wins, and make no mistake, that's exactly what it wants. Negativity thrives on doubt, feeds on fear and revels in pessimism. But the world needs your light. Your strength lies in standing tall, refusing to let the weight of negativity pull you under. When you shine, you create ripples of hope. You inspire. You ignite change. So, don't shrink. Don't stop. Shine brighter – you were born to light the way.

CHALLENGE

When negativity or doubt creeps in today, pause and reclaim your power. Choose one small action – start a creative project, speak your truth or do something that sparks joy – and let it remind you of your strength to shine brighter.

DAY 197: JUST GET HERE

However you get here today, just get here. Crawl, run, stumble –
whatever it takes to make it back to the drawing board. If you can
only show up as half of yourself, that's still better than not showing up
at all. Showing up is the hardest part, but it's also the most important.

Today is the movement. Today is the moment. This is the time you
decide to make it happen. It might take all day to find your focus or to
sit down and express yourself, but don't forget: you hold the power.
Every small step forward matters. Even when it feels like you're crawl-
ing, you're still moving. You don't have to have everything figured
out. You just have to show up. The rest will follow. In the end, you
decide what happens next.

CHALLENGE

Show up.

DAY 198: BE THE REASON

We get it – you need a reason. A reason to wake up in the morning, a reason to walk around the block, a reason to move your mind. But what if you stopped searching for reasons and instead built a reflex? A reflex that automatically moves you towards the things you know you need to do, without hesitation or excuse. The truth is, that kind of instinct comes from practice. You have to train your brain, again and again, to push through when it gets hard. The only way forward is through. So, stop waiting for the perfect reason – choose to act and watch yourself become the artist you've always known you could be.

CHALLENGE

Today, commit to taking one small creative action without waiting for the 'perfect' reason or ideal conditions. It could be writing a few lines, sketching an idea or brainstorming for 10 minutes. Focus on making it a reflex – something you do without hesitation.

DAY 199: FIND PEACE

Find peace in being misunderstood, in being overlooked, in being the one who sticks out. The more you wrestle with insecurity, the less time you spend working on your craft. You waste energy looking around, wondering why others aren't supporting you, questioning why they don't see your worth. But here's the truth: you don't need them to. Find peace in knowing they may never see your stuff, and that's okay. Peace is perspective. Peace is being able to move on, trusting that you're still growing, still creating, still moving forward. People are going to miss the boat, and that's not your problem. Be at peace with being your badass, unapologetic artist self – even if it means standing alone.

CHALLENGE

Today, write a letter to a part of yourself or a situation that has felt misunderstood or unresolved. Express your thoughts, frustrations and feelings without holding back. Then, allow yourself to let go of the burden, releasing any lingering resentment or confusion.

DAY 200: NAME IT TO KNOW IT

Name things so you know things. Naming is a form of creation – it's manifesting something into being, giving it space to exist. Why do we give names to humans? We're assigning them meaning, setting an intention for who they might become. Our art is the same. When you name your work, you're inviting it to take shape, assigning it a place in the world and a piece of your intention. A title – even a whispered word – gives form to what was once intangible. It's the act of making something known, claiming it as real. Give your ideas names. Name them so you can call them forth, make them concrete and watch as they transform from visions to creations, becoming exactly what they were meant to be.

CHALLENGE

Take one of your current projects or ideas – something that feels undefined or abstract – and give it a name. Even if it's temporary, let the act of naming it bring clarity and intention to what you're creating.

DAY 201: YOUR COMFORT ZONE IS A TRAP

Here's the deal: you're in the thick of it, feeling like your project is sucking the life out of you. Every little setback feels like a punch in the gut, and you can't shake that feeling of emptiness. But what if – just for a moment – you dared to see things differently? What if you flipped the script and saw that glass as half full instead of half empty?

Cosying up to sadness and wallowing in that negative energy is not doing you any favours. It's time to shake things up, break out of those comfort zones and start embracing a new mindset. It's worth it. All the magic happens on the other side of that discomfort. That's where you start to grow, learn, thrive.

CHALLENGE

- Get Uncomfortable: Challenge yourself to set ambitious creative goals that push you beyond your current skill level.
- Burst Your Bubble: Seek out opportunities to collaborate on projects or participate in creative communities where you can exchange feedback and inspiration with other creatives.
- Cross Boundaries: Sign up for workshops or classes in a creative discipline you've never explored before.
- Seek the Spark: Seek out new experiences and environments that stimulate your senses and spark your imagination.

DAY 202: PROTECT YOUR ART

Believe in your vision, even when others can't see it. The moment you find the courage to pursue your dreams, life will test you. Friends, family and even strangers may challenge you – intentionally or not – and it's in these moments that your strength is built. You'll need to set boundaries and stand firm in your convictions because your art is deeply personal. It's not just something you make; it's a reflection of who you are. Protect it fiercely. The struggle is part of the journey – let it shape you, drive you and inspire you to create something extraordinary.

CHALLENGE

Pick a part of your creative work where you've felt external pressure to conform or doubt from others. Instead of shrinking, lean into that resistance and create something that directly responds to it.

DAY 203: MENTAL HEALTH

We know you've been pouring everything into your craft, giving it your heart, your energy and your time. That kind of passion is inspiring, but even the most dedicated artist needs to step back and breathe. Your mind, that brilliant engine of ideas, deserves a moment to rest and recharge. Just like a canvas needs time to dry between layers, your creativity thrives when it's given space to refocus.

Taking a break isn't giving up – it's honouring yourself and your work. Rest fuels clarity, and clarity fuels brilliance. So, allow yourself to pause, to reset and to care for your mental well-being. Remember, you can't create your best work when you're running on empty. The world needs your vibrant energy, but it starts with you taking care of it. You've earned this moment – take it.

CHALLENGE

Do something for your mental peace today. That is the most important thing you can do for your creative brain.

DAY 204: LEAD BY EXAMPLE

Leading by example is more than just a concept – it's a way of showing what's possible. When you live the values you believe in, you create a ripple effect that inspires those around you. Your actions have the power to demonstrate what grit and dedication look like in practice, proving that the pursuit of your craft is worth the effort.

Instead of telling others what they can achieve, show them. Share your story with honesty. Embrace the challenges and victories that come with the journey. When you lead with heart and integrity, you build a community rooted in creativity and resilience. Your journey becomes a spark for others, encouraging them to pursue their dreams with the same courage. By leading through action, you empower others to find their own path forward.

CHALLENGE

How can you show your support to other creative friends today?

DAY 205: SPEAK IT INTO EXISTENCE

Return to this page whenever you need to.

I embrace my unique voice and express it freely through my art.
Every day, I nurture my creativity and let it grow in its own way.
I am deserving of success, joy and fulfilment in my creative work.
I trust the process and allow inspiration to come naturally.
My imagination is boundless; I am free to create without limits.
I draw inspiration from the world around me and channel it into meaningful work.
I celebrate every step forward, no matter how small, on my creative journey.
My art has the power to connect, heal and inspire others.
I trust my intuition and make bold choices with confidence.
I let go of the fear of judgement and create from a place of authenticity.
I welcome collaboration and the magic it brings to my work.
I honour my creative spirit by giving it the rest and renewal it needs to thrive.

CHALLENGE

Read this out loud.

DAY 206: CHOOSE TO BE

In the stillness, when doubt creeps in and the weight of the world feels unrelenting, we arrive at a pivotal moment. We can retreat into silence, letting fear stifle our voice, or we can choose courage. We can rise, open ourselves to the act of creating and let our ideas take shape. To create is to embrace vulnerability, to share what is raw and unpolished. This is where our truth lies – where our power begins. The world isn't waiting for perfection; it's waiting for your perspective, your story, your voice. Creation is not just an act of making – it's an act of being. To create is to say, 'I am here, and this is what I have to offer.'

So, when the crossroads appear, choose to be. Fully, boldly, unapologetically. Step into your creative potential with passion and faith. In creating, we don't just make art; we discover who we are. We light a path not only for ourselves but for others who might be searching for their own way forward. To create is to live.

CHALLENGE

Today, create something that boldly declares, 'I am here.' Write, draw or build something that reflects your unique voice and perspective, no matter how raw or unpolished it feels. Focus on expressing your truth, not perfection.

DAY 207: BREAK FREE

Creating for likes, clicks and shares isn't a true expression – it's chasing validation. The irony is hard to escape in a world where many are steeped in the internet's culture of metrics and algorithms. For creatives, the pressure to play this game can feel overwhelming, especially when it seems tied to professional success. But there is another way. What if you unplugged? What if you recentred and created solely for yourself? In that quiet space, free from the noise of external approval, something deeper emerges – peace, clarity and a connection to what truly matters. Yes, stepping out of the cycle of validation can feel isolating, and others may not understand your choice. But true creativity doesn't need to be understood by everyone; it needs to be honest, personal and free. In these moments of quiet creation, art transforms. It becomes a reflection of your journey, unshaped by others' expectations. And in that freedom, your truest voice is found.

CHALLENGE

Turn off your phone today.

DAY 208: COMMIT

Committing fully to the creative process brings a rare kind of freedom. It means embracing every moment – the triumphs, the setbacks and everything in between. Once a project is released into the world, it evolves from a deeply personal effort into something shared, open to interpretation. It no longer belongs solely to you but to those who experience it and find their own meaning in it. This is why the journey matters more than the outcome. The process is yours – unrushed, unfiltered and uniquely yours. Within it lies the space to grow, to explore and to discover who you are as an artist. Find peace in that commitment. When you honour the path you're on, your work carries authenticity and invites others to connect with it in a meaningful way. The more fully you show up for the journey, the more brightly your voice will shine.

CHALLENGE

Pick one step in your current project and share it with someone – whether it's a sketch, a draft or an idea you're working on. Invite them to connect with your process rather than the finished product and see how sharing this vulnerable moment deepens the meaning of your work.

DAY 209: STARTING OVER ISN'T GIVING UP

Starting over isn't the same as giving up, yet the two are so often mistaken for each other. As children, we're asked endlessly, 'What do you want to be when you grow up?' This question plants the idea that we should have life figured out – by secondary school, definitely by university and absolutely by graduation. But does anyone ever truly have it all figured out? The irony of growing older is realizing that life is full of people doing their best to navigate an unpredictable journey.

Starting over isn't failure – it's a courageous choice to realign with what feels true. It's an act of growth, a chance to explore paths that may lead to deeper clarity and purpose. The unknown can be intimidating, but it's also where creativity thrives. Let go of the pressure to follow a predetermined script. Instead, embrace the freedom to begin again, to pivot and to create a life that feels authentically yours – even if it diverges from what was expected.

CHALLENGE

Reflect on an area of your life or work that no longer feels aligned. Write down one way you could 'start over' or pivot to something that feels more true to you – no matter how small. Then, commit to taking one step towards that realignment, whether it's brainstorming, researching or starting fresh. Embrace the freedom to create your own path.

DAY 210: EMBRACE

Choosing a creative career often invites scepticism, especially from those on more traditional paths. Questions like, 'How will you make money?' or dismissive remarks about 'playing pretend' reveal a lack of understanding. Even the silence – the absence of likes, shares or support – can sting. But their doubts usually come from a place of concern, shaped by their own fears of failure. Pursuing a creative path is a bold declaration that you're forging your own way, and when the road gets rocky, the echoes of 'I told you so' may creep in. If you've lost the spark that once drove you – whether as a writer, designer or filmmaker – that's okay. Pause and reflect on what drew you to your craft in the first place. Was it the thrill of bringing ideas to life? The joy of creating something new? The satisfaction of being seen and understood through your work? There's power in the pivot. It's not about giving up; it's about recalibrating.

CHALLENGE

Rediscover what excites you, and let it lead you in a fresh direction. Creativity isn't a straight line – it's a winding path, and each turn is a chance to begin again.

DAY 211: LET LIFE SURPRISE YOU

You can't ever really have it all figured out. Every day brings a thousand micro-decisions that shape your journey without you even realizing it. Just look at Oprah Winfrey, who started as a news anchor before building her media empire, showing that a strong foundation can lead to greater heights. Dwayne 'The Rock' Johnson transitioned from wrestling to Hollywood stardom, proving that reinvention is possible at any stage in life. Vera Wang moved from figure skating and journalism to become a fashion icon, reminding us that passion can lead to unexpected places. So, while you may think you have everything mapped out today, let this serve as your reminder that you don't. Life is happening all around you! Breathe it in, stay open to possibilities and trust that your unique path is unfolding, one small decision at a time.

CHALLENGE

Take 10 minutes today to sketch out a 'path map' of your journey so far. Start with where you began and add the unexpected twists, decisions or moments that have shaped you. Then, leave space for the unknown – write or draw possibilities you might never have considered.

DAY 212: ANYONE CAN CREATE

If you've ever thought you're not 'creative enough', know this: creativity isn't reserved for a select few. Anyone has access to whatever they want in this life. You have the power to create and imagine anything in this world. Your imagination knows no bounds. If you feel the urge to create, listen to that calling. It doesn't matter if others have been at it longer or if they've mastered their artistic voice – your journey is your own, and you're just as worthy of creating as anyone else. Trust that your voice is unique and valuable, and the world needs to hear it.

CHALLENGE

Think of one creative urge or idea you've dismissed because you felt it wasn't 'worthy' or you weren't 'ready'. Take 20 minutes today to start it, even if it's messy or incomplete.

DAY 213: SIDE PROJECTS ARE STILL PROJECTS

Some seasons, the work that pays the bills may not spark your passion, but every step in the journey is essential. Research backs this up – creativity outside of work fuels everything else. A study from San Francisco State University found that people with creative side projects are not only more innovative but also more collaborative and helpful in their jobs. The mindset you bring to one part of your life impacts everything. So even if your side project feels small or separate, know that it's lighting up the rest of your world, fuelling your growth, joy and possibility. Keep creating – it's transforming you in ways you can't yet see.

CHALLENGE

Let Your Side Project Lead: Choose one task in your creative side project that excites you and let it guide your day. Approach your main work with the energy, perspective or inspiration that task sparked. Notice how the mindset from your passion project shifts how you tackle other responsibilities.

DAY 214: BE A SPONGE

Be a sponge – absorb everything. Every piece of content you consume, every moment of inspiration and everything happening around you is fuel for your creativity. Pay attention to the things that make you pause, the things you can't stop thinking about, and ask yourself why they resonate with you. Every experience, whether big or small, contributes to your unique perspective as a creator. The more you take in, the richer your creative expression will become. Soak it all up – it's part of shaping who you are and what you'll create next.

CHALLENGE

Curate Your Inspiration: Spend today intentionally observing the world around you. Write down three things that catch your attention – a piece of content, a conversation or a moment in your environment – and note why they resonate with you. At the end of the day, use one of these observations as a spark to create something new. Let what you absorb fuel your unique perspective.

DAY 215: DOPAMINE

Talking about your goals can feel like a win, giving you a burst of excitement, but don't let that fool you. It's tempting to share every idea and soak in the positive feedback, but sometimes those dopamine hits from talking can overshadow the satisfaction of execution. This isn't to say you can't discuss your goals – of course you can – but be mindful of the difference. Recognize when you're getting caught up in the hype of an idea rather than doing the work to make it real. The thrill of achievement doesn't come from dreaming; it comes from doing. Stay grounded, hold onto that quiet drive and let your actions speak louder than your words.

CHALLENGE

Choose one goal or idea that excites you. Write it down – what it is, why it matters and three steps you can take to make it real. Keep this plan to yourself and commit to completing one step before sharing it with anyone. Afterwards, reflect: did working in silence deepen your focus or spark new ideas? Let action, not talk, fuel your momentum.

DAY 216: WHAT'S YOUR AURA?

What kind of aura do you bring with you? Are you the person who lights up a room, who makes others feel comfortable, creative and alive? On set or in any creative space, energy is everything. The aura you carry can either spark inspiration or stifle it. Are you someone who brings good energy, who gives others a safe place to explore their ideas and push their boundaries? Creating isn't just about skill or talent – it's about the vibe you cultivate. When your presence encourages others to express themselves freely, you become more than just a collaborator; you become a catalyst for creativity. So, check in with yourself. What energy do you want to radiate? Make sure it's the kind that invites brilliance and builds trust, because that's the real magic of creative environments.

CHALLENGE

Write down three words that describe the vibe you want to radiate, e.g. supportive, vibrant, calm. As you work, notice how your presence influences others. Are you creating a safe, inspiring atmosphere? Afterwards, reflect on how your energy shaped the experience and how it felt to intentionally bring that aura into the room.

DAY 217: GAME CHANGER

Opening yourself to possibilities can transform your creative journey. Saying yes to new experiences invites unexpected opportunities. Take the meeting with someone you admire, even if you're unsure what to say. Follow the ideas that excite you and engage with those who inspire you – you never know how a simple connection might spark something extraordinary.

Embrace the uncertainty and let curiosity lead the way. Each interaction holds the potential to shift your path in ways you can't yet see. By welcoming these moments, you open the door to growth, collaboration and fresh perspectives. Step outside your comfort zone and watch as new possibilities unfold. The world is brimming with connections waiting to be discovered – are you ready to say yes?

CHALLENGE

This week, challenge yourself to say yes to one opportunity that feels exciting yet slightly outside your comfort zone. It could be reaching out to someone whose work you admire, attending a creative event or exploring an idea you've been hesitant to pursue.

DAY 218: ASSESS ENERGY

You have permission to try something new. You're not stuck. Just as you create worlds in your art, you can create a new reality for yourself. You're allowed to evolve, to step into something different and to pursue what calls to you now. The idea that you must remain the same or follow a set path is a myth. Reinvention is part of the creative process, and that applies to your life too. Assess the energy around you and keep moving. Some environments lift you up, others drain you – learn to tell the difference. Trying new things isn't just for your creative work; it's for your soul. Shake up your days, break out of your routines and seek change because you need it. Stagnation dulls your spirit, but change brings growth. Whether it's learning a new skill, meeting new people or simply shifting how you approach your day, keep evolving. Embrace the unknown – it's where your next breakthrough is waiting.

CHALLENGE

This week, break a routine or try something you've never done before – learn a skill, meet someone new or change how you approach your day. Notice how it shifts your energy and sparks fresh ideas. Small changes can lead to big breakthroughs.

DAY 219: STOP LYING

Lying as a creative is one of the quickest ways to sabotage your growth. When you desperately want to avoid something and resort to lying, you're not just deceiving others – you're cheating yourself. If you're feeling mentally unwell, be honest about it. But if you're avoiding the work, the connection and the discomfort that comes with creating, then you're missing the mark. Own your time and the commitments you've made. Rewiring your brain to stop procrastinating takes discipline, but it's necessary if you want to stay true to your craft. Lying is backtracking, and it's not only a betrayal to others but also a deep betrayal to yourself. Don't let yourself get comfortable with dishonesty. When you cheat yourself, you cheat your art.

CHALLENGE

Identify one task you've been avoiding. Commit to tackling it head-on this week, no excuses. Reflect on how it feels to honour your craft with honesty and follow-through.

DAY 220: HONOUR PEOPLE
AND THEIR TIME

Honouring other people's time is one of the simplest and most mean-ingful ways to show respect. The people around you are unique and valuable, even when your own chaos makes it easy to forget. If you find yourself annoyed or impatient, it's time to check your empathy. Are you truly seeing them for who they are? Their time, energy and efforts matter just as much as your own.

We're all busy, but mutual respect is the foundation of meaning-ful connections. As creatives, empathy is part of our calling. It allows us to create with love, understanding and humanity – even if that sounds a little mushy.

CHALLENGE

Today, honour someone's time and energy – whether by listening fully, showing up on time or offering grace. Notice how small acts of respect deepen your connections.

DAY 221: DON'T LET ANXIETY TAKE THE WHEEL

Don't let anxiety take the wheel. We get it – creating something that exists in the future makes it hard to live in the now. The fear of what's ahead or not measuring up can pull you out of the present moment. But remember, the work happening right now is paving the way for the future you desire. The process, with all its uncertainty and chaos, is where the magic happens. Creativity isn't just about the end result; it's about being present enough to let inspiration find you. So how do we stay grounded when the best art often comes from stepping outside our minds? Trust the flow. Stay in the now. That's where the breakthrough happens.

CHALLENGE

Set a timer for 15 minutes and create something without worrying about the outcome – write, draw or brainstorm freely. Focus only on the act of creating, not the result. Reflect afterwards: how did staying in the present moment shape your process?

DAY 222: THERE IS ALWAYS A WAY

There is always a way. Have you forgotten the chase? That intoxicating feeling of yearning for someone's attention or, even more, the thrill of chasing your art? Remember when nothing could stand in your way – when every obstacle felt like a challenge, not a reason to stop? But somewhere along the way, you confused needing rest with being apathetic. Rest is important, but don't let it blur into indifference. That fire you had still burns inside you. The passion, the pursuit – it's all there, waiting for you to reclaim it. There's always a way forward if you remember why you started.

CHALLENGE

Reconnect with your passion by writing down why you started your creative journey. Then, take one action today – no matter how small – that reminds you of the thrill of creating. Let that spark guide you forward.

DAY 223: BE THE AVALANCHE

Creativity is like an avalanche – one small moment sets everything else in motion. The more you create, the more momentum you build. Each step, each idea, each project adds layers, growing bigger and faster with each push. This practice of creating and repeating is that snowball: it keeps rolling, unstoppable, because once you're in motion, you can't let it all melt away. What you're building isn't just about you – it's a force that's bigger than you, expanding with every piece you create. Keep pushing, keep building and watch your creativity grow.

CHALLENGE

Choose one small creative action you can take today – a sketch, a sentence, a photo, anything. Commit to repeating this action tomorrow and the next day, letting it build momentum.

DAY 224: STAY HUMBLE

Stay humble. No matter how far you go, always leave room for the artist with questions – the one who looks up to what you've built. There will come a time when you're no longer the newcomer; you'll be the veteran. And how you treat others on your way up will leave a lasting impact. Your kindness, your grace and your willingness to lend a hand can shape someone else's journey.

Be the person you once needed – the one who lifts others up, answers the questions and believes in them before they believe in themselves. Remember, success isn't just about how high you climb; it's about how many people you help raise along the way. Keep your heart open, your ego in check and never forget that giving back is the true mark of greatness.

CHALLENGE

This week, take time to support someone who's just starting out. Answer a question, share advice or simply offer encouragement.

DAY 225: OWN UP TO YOUR MISTAKES

Own up to your mistakes in the creative process. You won't always be an A-plus, and that's okay – you're human. Mistakes will happen, not just artistic ones but technical ones, too. Maybe you submit the wrong design to the screen printer and end up with 100 misprinted hoodies. It happens. The only thing you can and should do is own the mistake and find a way to fix it. That mindset shouldn't just be your approach to art; it should be a life motto. Owning up to your mess-ups and making them right is how you grow, how you evolve and how you build trust in yourself and with others. You are still talented and amazing with mistakes. Life moves on. Trust us.

CHALLENGE

Think back to a creative mistake you've made – big or small. Reflect on what you learned from it and write down one way it helped you grow. This week, if a new mistake happens, own it immediately and brainstorm a creative solution. Remember, mistakes are part of the process, not the end of it.

DAY 226: GIVE A LITTLE MORE

Real growth happens when you step beyond what feels comfortable. You've hit your quota for the day, but there's still a little fire left in the tank. The question is, will you use it? Breakthroughs often come when you're willing to go the extra mile, stay a little longer and push yourself past what feels like enough. This is grit. This is where resilience is built and horizons expand. Growth doesn't come from staying in your comfort zone – it comes from pushing through the moments when stopping feels easier. Today, give a little more. Push a little further. You might surprise yourself.

CHALLENGE

Today, when you feel like stopping, give a little more – whether it's 5 extra minutes, one more idea or an additional step forward. Reflect on how it feels to push past your usual limits and what breakthroughs, big or small, come from that extra effort.

DAY 227: GROWING OR FADING

You've been on this journey for a while now, and that's a good thing. You're starting to understand what it takes to become the version of yourself you've always dreamed of. The real truth about this transformation is that it's a process of becoming. You don't just reach your destination and stop; you continually evolve. Just like a flower doesn't bloom and freeze in time, you're either growing or fading. Embrace the fact that every moment contributes to your growth. Celebrate where you are now, knowing that each step forward is a vital part of your ongoing journey. Remember, it's not about perfection; it's about progression.

CHALLENGE

Write down three ways you've grown or evolved recently. Then, set one small goal to keep moving forward – not for perfection, but for progress. Celebrate every step.

DAY 228: REPEAT

I believe in myself. I believe in myself.

CHALLENGE

Believe in yourself today.

DAY 229: CREATE SPACE

Finding what you're missing isn't about waiting for inspiration to strike; it's about persistence and intention. You have to commit to not quitting, even when the path seems unclear. Creating space for that elusive thing requires more than just desire; it demands action.

Get everything in line and prepare for the expansion that's about to come. Think of it this way: you can't wish for a bountiful vegetable garden without first cultivating the soil and planting the seeds. Similarly, you can't hope for growth in your life without laying the groundwork for it. Take the time to clear away the clutter – both mentally and physically – and make room for the possibilities that await. The universe responds to those who are ready to receive, so make sure you're prepared for the abundance that is sure to follow. Embrace the journey of finding and remember: your best work is often just around the corner, waiting for you to discover it.

CHALLENGE

Take 15 minutes today to clear space – physically or mentally – for the growth you're seeking. Organize your workspace, journal about what you want to achieve or let go of one distraction holding you back. Set the stage for inspiration to arrive and take the first step towards your next breakthrough.

DAY 230: READ ME IF YOU'RE READY TO SET YOUR OWN PATH

Life isn't about following a script someone else wrote for you. It's about questioning, exploring and redefining what truly matters – no matter where you are in your journey.

Every moment is an opportunity to push boundaries, challenge norms and discover what resonates with you. The last thing you want is to wake up one day and realize you spent your life meeting expectations that weren't your own. **So, take ownership.** Experiment, take risks and lean into the things that make you feel alive.

And this isn't just for a specific season of life – it's for anyone, at any age, who is ready to step into their power. Reinvention has no expiration date. Creativity, curiosity and the courage to start fresh are always within reach. Your story is yours to write, erase and rewrite as many times as you need. Make sure the life you're living is one that feels like home.

CHALLENGE

Write about how this 'unfinished' stage is shaping you – what you're learning, how you're growing and what possibilities it holds. Remind yourself that the journey itself is where the magic happens.

DAY 231: BE SELFISH

What if we allowed ourselves to be a little selfish, in the best way possible? Being 'self-love selfish' means tuning into your own needs and letting them take priority. It means creating what feels true to you, without constantly checking if it fits someone else's mould. Sometimes we overextend ourselves not because we deeply care, but because we're afraid of what will happen if we stop. We worry we'll lose favour, opportunities or validation. But that kind of energy isn't sustainable, and people can sense when you're giving from an empty place. As a creative, putting yourself first isn't just an act of self-care; it's a way to protect your craft. When you prioritize your well-being, your art thrives. You become more present, more authentic and more capable of bringing something real into the world. So, let yourself be a little selfish. Create from a place that feels true to you, even if it means saying 'no' more often. Your peace matters, and it's what fuels your best work.

CHALLENGE

This week, say no to one thing that drains your energy and yes to something that nurtures you – whether it's dedicating time to a personal project, resting or simply enjoying a moment of peace.

DAY 232: RELEASE THE PRESSURE

Creatives are a lot like pressure cookers. We're constantly taking in ideas, emotions and inspirations, letting them build up inside. There's this intense energy, a bubbling under the surface that's just waiting to be released. But here's the thing about a pressure cooker: if you don't let the steam out, it will explode. The creative process can feel exactly like that. We put so much pressure on ourselves to perform, to produce, to be perfect, that we forget to release the valve and let out some of that built-up tension. But that kind of intensity isn't sustainable – it's not how beautiful, honest work gets made. Releasing the steam doesn't mean letting go of the drive; it means finding healthy outlets, taking a break, and allowing yourself to breathe. Today, you need to breathe. Remember, the most flavourful meals are the ones cooked just right, not rushed or forced, but given the time they need to come together. Your art deserves that kind of care too.

CHALLENGE

Today, take 10 minutes to release the creative pressure. Go for a walk, journal freely or do something that clears your mind and resets your energy. Reflect on how it feels to let go of tension and how it might bring clarity or ease to your process. Remember, great work comes from balance, not burnout.

DAY 233: STEP IN AND STEP UP

Sometimes, the work just finds you. The kind of work you didn't ask for but always dreamed of. It's like the universe has been quietly conspiring and now, without warning, the opportunity you thought was out of reach has been dropped right in your lap. Almost like it was waiting for you to be ready. And here's the beauty of it: you don't have to fight for it or prove yourself in some exhausting, uphill battle. You just have to step up and step into it. Sometimes, it really is that simple. You've spent years doubting yourself, playing small and second-guessing every move. But what if, just for today, you chose to believe? What if, today, you trusted that the work that came to you was yours to do? When you step into your calling with confidence, you find out it's been waiting for you all along.

CHALLENGE

Think about an opportunity or idea that's come your way recently – something that excites you but also makes you doubt if you're ready. Today, act on it. Take one small step forward with confidence, trusting that it's yours to do. Reflect on how it feels to embrace what's been waiting for you.

DAY 234: PLAN FOR SUCCESS

This journey isn't just about what you create – it's about who you become along the way. Success isn't something you stumble into; it's something you prepare for. You're not waiting for a lucky break; you're laying the foundation, crafting a path that leads directly to the life you've envisioned.

This is your moment to step forward with intention, to claim your space and use your voice with purpose. Every choice you make brings you closer to your vision. The success you're seeking isn't hiding – it's waiting for you to take action.

CHALLENGE

Identify one bold step you can take today towards the life you're building – whether it's outlining a project, reaching out for an opportunity or simply declaring your intention to yourself.

DAY 235: TIME TO DREAM AGAIN

Give yourself permission to dream again. It's time to shake off the weight of disappointment and reignite that spark within you. Creativity can feel like a rollercoaster, filled with highs and lows, and it's easy to fall into the trap of self-blame when certain paths don't lead where you hoped they would. But remember, just because one door closed doesn't mean the house is empty. Your potential isn't tied to past failures; it's tied to the dreams you still hold. Give yourself the space to believe in your vision once more. Think about all the possibilities that lie ahead, the projects that excite you and the goals that once made your heart race. Allow yourself to dream of success without the weight of your past on your shoulders. Each disappointment is just a stepping stone, not a stop sign. When you give yourself permission to envision new heights, you reclaim your power.

CHALLENGE

Take 10 minutes to write down a dream or goal you've been afraid to revisit. Let go of past disappointments and imagine it with fresh eyes. What excites you about it? What small step could you take towards it today? Allow yourself to dream freely, knowing that your potential isn't defined by past outcomes.

DAY 236: BE VULNERABLE

Vulnerability is a powerful force in the creative journey. When you share your true self and create from a place of sincerity – free from the pull of personal gain – people feel that honesty. They're drawn to it. They want to support it. Vulnerability in your art isn't a weakness; it's what gives it life. Be open about what you want to say and how you want to say it. That rawness is where connection happens, where your work begins to resonate and take on meaning beyond yourself.

By allowing yourself to be seen, flaws and all, you create space for others to do the same. Your truth becomes a mirror, inviting others to reflect on their own stories and join you on the journey. So, let your heart lead. Embrace the messy, the raw and the real in your creativity. That's where the magic lives.

CHALLENGE

Go be vulnerable with a stranger. Strike up a real conversation with someone you don't normally talk to – a barista, a coworker, a neighbour whose name you don't know. Share something honest. It doesn't have to be deep, just real. See what happens when you let your guard down.

DAY 237: PASSION AND PROFIT

Creating for passion and profit often feels like a tightrope walk, balancing artistic expression with the need for financial stability. On one hand, your passion drives you to create authentically, pouring your heart into your art. On the other, the pressure to monetize can stifle that creativity, leading to compromises that feel disingenuous. However, passion and profit can coexist. When you create from a place of authenticity, your work resonates more deeply, opening doors to opportunities that align with your values. Embrace innovative ways to share your art, like collaborations or workshops, that reflect your unique perspective while generating income. Ultimately, the dance between passion and profit is dynamic. Today, embrace the tension, trusting that your voice has value. With persistence, you can carve out a space that honours both your creative spirit and financial aspirations.

CHALLENGE

Think of one way you can share your art authentically while creating an opportunity for income. It could be brainstorming a workshop, offering a collaboration or showcasing your work in a new space. Take one small step today to bring that idea closer to reality. Reflect on how it feels to honour both your creativity and your financial goals.

DAY 238: DON'T STAY THE SAME

Today is the perfect day to break free from the familiar. While routine offers comfort, it can also lead to stagnation, dulling your ability to empathize and connect with the world around you. Growth comes from stepping into the unknown, whether that's taking a new route, reading a book outside your usual genre or starting a conversation with someone who sees the world differently.

Empathy flourishes when we let ourselves experience life through fresh perspectives. The discomfort of the unfamiliar is a powerful teacher – it stretches your heart and sharpens your creative vision. So, dare to do something different today. Lean into the unknown. Your creative spirit will grow and your capacity for connection will deepen. Your future self will thank you for it.

CHALLENGE

Today, do one thing differently. Take a new route, try a new activity or engage with someone outside your usual circle. Do anything and feel the burst of potential.

DAY 239: SHOW UP TODAY

You have a choice to show up differently today. In fact, you must show up differently today. Whether you're stepping onto a set, walking into an office or popping into your kitchen, your attitude needs to be a solid 10. Today is the day to declare, 'We are doing this, no matter what!' Embrace the power of your presence. You have the ability to will things into existence simply because you're determined to make them happen. No more holding back or letting self-doubt creep in. This is your moment to shine, to push through any obstacles and to bring your unique vision to life. So, step into your space with confidence, knowing that your energy can transform not just your day but the world around you. Let this be the day you ignite your passion and unleash your creativity. Show up and stand tall.

CHALLENGE

Before starting your creative work today, take a moment to set an intention: how do you want to show up? Write it down or say it out loud. Then, step into your space – whether it's a studio, office or kitchen – with confidence and determination.

DAY 240: TREE OF LIFE

Before you get too far ahead of yourself today with excuses, take a moment to observe the tree outside your window. This tree stands resilient, unwavering through every storm, every burst of sunshine and every season. It doesn't get to choose its circumstances; it simply remains rooted in its purpose. Just like that tree, you, as a creative, have your own steadfastness. You may face challenges and uncertainties, but your commitment to your craft is what defines you. When those winds of doubt start swirling, think about that tree and how it offers shade to anyone looking for a break. Your creativity does the same thing – it can be a safe haven for others. Those leaves dancing in the breeze? They're just like your ideas, providing nourishment and comfort to everyone who comes across your work.

So, ground yourself in your purpose today. Embrace the storms and the sunshine, and continue to create and share, knowing that like that tree, you are a vital part of the ecosystem around you.

CHALLENGE

Write down what drives you to create and how your work offers shade, comfort or inspiration to others. Then, commit to one action today – no matter how small – that aligns with that purpose.

DAY 241: CREATE WITHOUT LIMITS

Let's keep it simple. Life is full of rules, but your art is where freedom lives. Forget the expectations, let go of the constraints and embrace the beautiful chaos of creativity. The only rule is to express yourself authentically.

CHALLENGE

Let go of the pressure to get it 'right' today. Just be, just create and let your expression flow without overthinking. Whether it's a doodle, a note or a dance, let yourself play. This isn't about perfection – it's about enjoying the act of creating.

DAY 242: TODAY MUST COUNT

You can't afford to miss another day. Not now, not ever. You can't keep putting off your creativity, telling yourself you'll do it tomorrow. That excuse has run its course. Today is the day you show up, no matter how messy or imperfect it feels. You owe it to yourself to close the circle, to finish what you've started. Every moment you wait is a moment lost, and there are no shortcuts around that. The only way through is to step up and do the work, today. Not because it's easy, but because it matters. You've got a vision inside you and it's time to bring it to life. No more waiting, no more skipping days.

CHALLENGE

Today is the day you commit to making it happen. How you do it is up to you – just make the choice and go for it.

DAY 243: HAPPY + SAD

The opposite of depression isn't happiness – it's expression. This perspective reshapes how we approach the journey out of depressive feelings. Instead of striving for an often elusive sense of happiness, it suggests that the real antidote lies in finding ways to express what we're feeling, rather than forcing ourselves to feel something else.

Expression, particularly through art, provides an outlet for emotions we might otherwise suppress or bury. It's about giving voice to what's inside, no matter how messy, painful or raw. In doing so, we acknowledge our emotions and experiences – a crucial step towards understanding and healing.

This approach shifts the focus from chasing happiness to taking meaningful, tangible action. It's about allowing ourselves to be seen and heard, embracing authenticity over avoidance. Expression becomes the bridge between where we are and where we want to be, offering a path to connection, understanding and, ultimately, growth.

CHALLENGE

Don't worry about how it looks or sounds; focus on letting it out. Reflect on how it feels to acknowledge and release your emotions through your creativity.

DAY 244: OPEN YOUR HEART

Being vulnerable in your art isn't just about showing what you've made; it's about revealing who you are. It's raw, it's real, and sometimes it feels like standing in front of the world with your heart wide open. But maybe that's exactly the point. Maybe the push you're resisting – the one that feels a little too close, a little too personal – is precisely what will set you free.

Vulnerability is where true artistry lives. It's where your work stops being just a collection of pretty things and starts to mean something deeper. Because when you strip away the layers and share your fears, your hopes and your struggles, you're not just making art; you're creating a bridge. You're giving people a chance to see themselves in your story, to feel connected, understood and less alone.

CHALLENGE

Create something that feels personal and raw – a piece that reveals a part of who you are. Focus on expressing your fears, hopes or struggles without filtering or holding back. If you feel ready, share it with someone and reflect on how vulnerability deepens the meaning of your work and its connection to others.

DAY 245: SAY WHO YOU WANT TO BE

1. I AM Capable: Even on the days when I feel uncertain, I have everything I need to move forward. I am equipped to handle what comes my way.
2. I AM Resilient: I can bend without breaking. I rise up, time and time again, because I believe in my purpose.
3. I AM Creative: My mind is a well of endless ideas. I am open to new inspiration and ready to bring my visions to life.
4. I AM Worthy: I deserve to take up space, to share my voice and to see my dreams realized.
5. I AM Brave: I choose courage over comfort. I step into the unknown because I know there's growth on the other side.
6. I AM Grateful: I recognize the beauty in what I already have, even as I strive for more. Gratitude fuels my journey.
7. I AM Evolving: I am always in the process of becoming. I welcome change because it's how I grow into who I'm meant to be.
8. I AM Focused: I am clear on my intentions, and I give my energy to what truly matters.
9. I AM Learning: I am open to new lessons and wisdom, and I see every experience as an opportunity to grow.
10. I AM Enough: Exactly as I am, without needing to prove or pretend. I am worthy, valuable and complete.

CHALLENGE

Read this out loud.

DAY 246: FIND THE LIGHT

Fear is loud, but it doesn't define you. It doesn't know the depth of your potential or the power of your vision. Fear can't see the magic that happens when you create from the truest, freest part of yourself. You are not held back by doubt – you are driven by passion, purpose and an unshakeable belief in what you can bring to life. Fear wants to keep you small, tucked away in the shadows. But creativity thrives in the light. It grows when you take bold risks, embrace mistakes and rise stronger each time you try again. So, step forward. Show fear it has no claim over your brilliance. Let your courage lead the way and watch your creativity soar.

CHALLENGE

Take a moment to write down what fear is telling you today. Be specific – what is it trying to stop you from doing? Then, counter it by writing one truth about your creative potential. Keep this truth visible as you create, and let it drown out the noise of doubt.

DAY 247: YOU NEVER KNOW

The best part of this creative life is the beautiful unpredictability of it all. You truly never know what's coming next. You're just one call away from everything changing, one email away from that long-awaited 'yes' that could open doors you never thought possible. It's this uncertainty, this wild possibility, that keeps the fire alive. So, keep holding on, even on the days when it feels like nothing is moving. Keep showing up, even when the road feels long and winding. Because all it takes is one moment, one connection, one spark to shift everything. The magic of a creative life lies in the fact that every day is a chance for something incredible to unfold. You're always on the brink of a breakthrough – stay ready, stay hopeful and keep creating and repeating.

CHALLENGE

Today, approach your creative work with the excitement that anything can happen. Write down one bold opportunity you'd love to receive – a dream project, collaboration or breakthrough moment. Then, take one action that aligns with that vision: send an email, refine your portfolio or share your work.

DAY 248: PLEASE

Please. Today, just please. Please let today be the day you allow yourself a burst of creative joy, the kind that lights you up from the inside out. Please let go of your fears, the ones that whisper doubt and keep you small. Please, just be. Be in this moment, without the weight of everything else. Please rest, let yourself breathe without guilt or rush. Please create, not because you have to but because you want to – because it feels good to make something that didn't exist before. And then, please repeat. Again and again, with all the love and passion you can muster. Don't make us beg – just, please. Let today be the day you say yes to yourself.

CHALLENGE

Choose one small thing to say yes to today – whether it's rest, play or making something just for you. Let it be a gentle act of self-permission.

DAY 249: YOU WILL ALWAYS BE TOO TIRED

You will always be tired. Do you see how lame that is? There will always be a reason, an excuse, a moment where you think, 'I can't possibly push through one more hour.' But the truth? Your soul is begging you to dig deeper, to give just a little more, to invest that extra ounce of energy into your creative breakthrough. This grind, this exhaustion – it's not a roadblock; it's the path. The life of a professional, working creative is on the other side of this effort. It's the late nights, the extra hours, the times you push past tiredness that build the momentum for everything you've dreamed of. So, when you're tempted to give in, remember: one more hour could be the hour that changes everything.

CHALLENGE

When you feel tempted to stop today, commit to one extra hour of focused creative work. Use this time to tackle something you've been putting off or to refine an idea you've been excited about.

DAY 250: LET ANGER DRIVE YOU

Distractions, disappointments and annoyances are bound to show up. Work through them. Let the dysfunction fuel your creative chaos and keep chasing the moment. If you're on camera, be honest – share what's happening and invite your audience into the process.

Frustration isn't a detour; it's part of the journey. It's often in those messy, unpredictable moments that true creativity is born. Don't shy away from it – channel it. Let the setbacks ignite something raw and real within you, and let that become your art.

CHALLENGE

Let the messiness of the day become part of the process. Embrace the imperfection and reflect: how did working through the chaos spark something unexpected?

DAY 251: EYES OF GIANTS

Have you ever looked into the eyes of a creature far larger than your-self? We're not talking about your dog or cat. I mean elephant-sized. There's a stillness that overtakes you in that moment, as if time slows just enough for the universe to say hello. You realize how small you are, and in that smallness, how connected you become to something infinitely larger. You are part of a much grander, intricate tapestry. In that shift, you find humility. And in humility, you rediscover the raw, unpolished truth that creativity often hides in the moments where you aren't trying to control it. Maybe you need the reminder that your story isn't the only one unfolding. You can stop pushing for a moment and just be. And when you are no longer the main charac-ter, you are free to create with reckless abandon – free to tap into the world beyond yourself.

CHALLENGE

Step Outside and Observe: Spend 10 minutes outside today, focusing on something larger than yourself – a tree, the sky or even the rhythm of a bustling city. Reflect on how it feels to be a small part of a vast, interconnected world. Let this perspective influence your next creative project.

DAY 252: SILENCE SPEAKS VOLUMES

In a world full of noise, what happens when you create from silence? How can moments of complete stillness spark the loudest ideas? There's something profound that happens in stillness. It strips away the distractions and you're left with just yourself and the raw material of your imagination. When you sit in silence, your mind becomes a blank canvas, ready to absorb the subtlest cues. The loudest ideas aren't always the ones that shout – they often arrive in whispers, gently nudging you forward. In these moments, when the world quiets down, you begin to hear what's been waiting to surface all along. The inner voice you've ignored, the fleeting thoughts that never had a chance to breathe.

CHALLENGE

Be quiet. That's all.

DAY 253: THE ART OF FORGETTING

Can forgetting past mistakes and old ideas be a creative act? What new things come to life when you let go of what you think you know? When you forget, you're not erasing yourself; you're freeing yourself from the weight of old stories. You stop living by the rules you once set and open up to new possibilities. Forgetting doesn't mean abandoning your experiences – it means letting go of the control they have over your future creations. When you let go of what you think you know, you allow your instincts to guide you, leading you down paths you might never have walked before. You no longer need to be tethered to what worked or didn't work before. Become the explorer again.

CHALLENGE

Take a moment to reflect on an old idea, rule or past mistake that's been holding you back. Write it down, then physically let it go – crumple the paper, tear it up or toss it away. Now, create something new, letting your instincts guide you.

DAY 254: BLUR REALITY

Today, let's step out of the confines of reality. Yes, vulnerability is powerful, but so is make-believe. What if the truest form of creative freedom lies not in expressing what is, but in embracing what could be? What if the key to your next breakthrough is in playing pretend? When you allow yourself to play pretend, you let go of the constraints of logic, of what's 'real', and give yourself permission to express the wildest, most impossible ideas. In these alternate realities, you can be whoever you want to be. You can create without fear because here, nothing is too far-fetched. The beauty of stepping outside reality is that you don't have to stay there forever. You can bring pieces of that imagined world back with you – tiny fragments of wonder and possibility that transform how you see the real world. The boundaries are yours to break.

CHALLENGE

Close your eyes and envision a world where anything is possible – no rules, no boundaries, just pure creativity. What does this world look like? What are its rules, its colours, its sounds? Now, bring one element of this imagined space to life.

DAY 255: LEAN INTO THE VOID

Have you ever stared at a blank page or canvas and felt that knot of fear tightening in your chest? That fear is real. It whispers doubts: 'What if I can't fill this? What if what I create isn't good enough?' But what if, instead of seeing the void as a threat, you welcomed it as an invitation? A blank page is pure potential. It's not demanding perfection; it's asking you to explore. It's an open space where your ideas can take shape – where your imagination can run wild. The emptiness you feel isn't a signal of failure. It's a starting point, a space waiting for you to breathe life into it. When you feel empty, it's easy to think you have nothing to give, but that's when the most unexpected magic happens. In emptiness, there are no limits, no preconceived notions of what *should* be. So, lean into the void. We dare you.

CHALLENGE

Welcome the void today.

DAY 256: CREATING IS ALSO LISTENING

What if creating is your way of communicating with the universe, with life itself? It's easy to think of creativity as a deeply personal act, an outpouring of your thoughts and emotions. But what if it's more than that? What if creating is also about listening – tuning into something larger than yourself? A force, a flow, an intuition that moves through you and out into the world. When you create, it's not just you speaking; it's you responding. Your art becomes a bridge to the unknown, a way of reaching beyond what you know and stepping into possibilities you've yet to imagine. It's an act of expansion, a way to break past your own limitations and tap into something infinite – ideas, emotions and dreams waiting to be discovered.

CHALLENGE
Pause and ask: what are you reaching for? What's reaching back?

DAY 257: LET GO AGAIN

Not every idea needs to live. It's a hard truth to face, but one that holds immense power. As creatives, we often fall in love with our ideas – each one feels precious, as if letting go means losing part of ourselves. But what if the real act of creation isn't in clinging to every spark, but in knowing when to release them? Letting an idea go doesn't mean it wasn't worthy. It simply means it wasn't the right time or maybe it wasn't the right shape. There's a subtle beauty in this process. Releasing an idea creates room for growth, not just for your work but for yourself. Often, the best ideas emerge not when you try to force them into existence, but when you create the space for them to unfold naturally. Letting go is an act of trust – in yourself, in the creative process and in the belief that more ideas will always come.

CHALLENGE

So, when you feel stuck or when an idea isn't working, ask yourself: is this one of the ideas that doesn't need to live? And what might blossom when I let it go?

DAY 258: DO AS NATURE DOES

What does nature teach you about timing and rhythm in your creative process? Look around – nature never rushes, yet everything gets done. Trees grow at their own pace, the tides ebb and flow and the seasons shift with quiet certainty. There's a wisdom in that rhythm, one that speaks to the heart of creation. Nature moves in cycles, not in straight lines. Some days are for planting seeds, while others are for letting them lie dormant, waiting for the right moment to bloom. Creativity works in the same way. There are seasons for growth and expansion, where ideas burst forth with energy; and seasons for rest and reflection, where stillness becomes just as important as action. Which one are you in right now?

CHALLENGE

Go outside, or simply sit by a window, and observe nature for a few minutes. Notice its pace, its stillness, its movement. Embrace the season you're in and create without pressure, just as nature does.

DAY 259: ELEMENTS

The elements – earth, water, fire and air – each hold a lesson for the creative soul.

Earth teaches patience and grounding. It reminds you that growth takes time and that laying a solid foundation is key to lasting creations. Water shows you how to adapt and flow. Creativity doesn't always follow a straight path; it moves, shifts and changes direction, and that's where its beauty lies. Fire sparks passion and drive. It fuels you to take bold risks, burn away the old and make space for something new. Air lifts your imagination, teaching you to dream big, to think beyond boundaries and to let your ideas soar. Together, the elements remind you that creativity is a dance – sometimes grounded, sometimes fluid, sometimes fiery, and always full of possibility. EMBRACE.

CHALLENGE

Choose one element – earth, water, fire or air – and let it inspire your creative work today. Whether it's grounding yourself with earthy textures, flowing freely like water in your process, igniting bold ideas with fire or letting your imagination soar like air, channel its energy into what you create.

DAY 260: BOUNDARIES

Sometimes, you need rules. Boundaries give you a structure to work within. You can't just float aimlessly in the vast expanse of ideas, hoping your feet will eventually touch the ground. Boundaries, whether they're deadlines, limited resources or tight constraints, are not roadblocks – they're the framework that pushes you to create. Think about it: the uni essay due at 6 a.m., the art project with a limited budget or the short time you had to pull together a last-minute idea. These moments of pressure force you to focus, to cut through the noise of endless possibilities and to find a solution within the space you're given. It's often within these limitations that your most original work is born. You need to learn to transform the limitations into opportunities.

CHALLENGE

Choose one creative project and impose a constraint on yourself – set a time limit, use only specific materials or work with a minimal budget. Embrace the challenge of working within these boundaries and see how it sharpens your focus and sparks originality.

DAY 261: ART AS A MIRROR, ART AS A WINDOW

Do you create to reflect who you are or to uncover something beyond yourself? Art can be a mirror, revealing your inner world – your emotions, thoughts and truths, even the ones you didn't know were there. But art can also be a window, offering a glimpse into new worlds, fresh perspectives and uncharted ideas. When you only create as a reflection, you stay in the world of the familiar. But when you create to explore, you step into the unknown, breaking your own rules and pushing past the limits you once thought defined you. This is where true growth happens, where creativity transforms into discovery. Art doesn't have to choose – it can be both a mirror and a window. It can ground you in who you are while guiding you towards what's possible.

CHALLENGE

Is your art holding up a mirror to your soul or opening a window to something new?

DAY 262: THE POWER OF ACCOUNTABILITY

You need that person who holds you to a higher standard. The one who knows you're supposed to be writing every day and checks in on that process. It's not to be annoying – it's to be a guiding light, reminding you of the commitment you've made to yourself. You need that push. Accountability isn't about pressure; it's about growth. It's about having a community that believes in your potential and keeps you moving when it gets hard. When someone checks in, it's a sign they see what you're capable of, even on the days when you can't. To grow, you have to do the things you say you're going to do. Sometimes, that means letting others hold you to it. The accountability you build with others creates a space where you not only show up but push yourself beyond what you thought possible.

CHALLENGE

Take a moment today to identify one person or group who can hold you to a higher standard, someone who believes in your potential and will check in on your progress. Reach out to them and share one goal you're working towards, asking them to help you stay accountable.

DAY 263: YOUR SPACE, YOUR MIND

What does your creative space say about your mind? Is it chaotic, cluttered, or calm and organized? The environment you create shapes more than just the work – it shapes the process itself. A space full of distractions reflects a mind full of noise. But a space that feels intentional can clear the path for new ideas. Your space is a mirror of where you are mentally. When you design a space that feels inspiring, it's easier to step into your creative flow. The way you arrange your tools, the light that filters in, even the objects you keep around you – they all influence how you think, how you create and what comes out of that process.

CHALLENGE

So, look around. What is your space telling you? And how can it be a place that encourages the kind of work you want to create?

DAY 264: QUIET VICTORY

Pause. Feel the weight of your work – not as exhaustion, but as pride. Today, you shaped something out of nothing, no matter the size or scale. Accomplishment doesn't always come with applause; it often happens quietly, when no one is watching. This is one of those moments. You made choices, you moved forward. It may not have been perfect, and it may not have been easy, but it was yours. Progress is rarely loud; it's like a seed growing underground, unseen but alive with possibility. Tonight, honour the roots you've planted, even if the bloom is yet to come. Give yourself permission to rest – not because the work is finished, but because it's already growing. You've done enough today. Trust that.

CHALLENGE

Honour Your Progress: Take 5 minutes tonight to reflect on what you accomplished today. Write down one thing – big or small – that moved you forward. Then, intentionally rest, knowing your efforts are already taking root. Trust that progress, even when it's quiet, is still progress.

DAY 265: BACK TO YOUR ROOTS

Go back. Not just in memory, but to the physical space – the place that first sparked something inside you. Put your feet in the same sand you played in as a kid. Feel the ground beneath you, the beach shore where the air was thick with salt and the world felt endless. These moments, these physical elements, shaped your creativity long before you knew what it meant to create.

The feeling of home is more than a memory; it's something tangible. It's in the scent of the ocean, the sound of birds in the distance, the texture of weathered wood beneath your hands. When you reconnect with these pieces of your past, you reconnect with yourself – the part of you that creates from a place of instinct, curiosity and safety. If you can't get there physically, let your senses take you. Taste something familiar, listen to the sounds of home or breathe in a scent that anchors you. These small moments can transport you back to that feeling of home, grounding you in your creativity once again.

CHALLENGE

Today, let the familiar guide you. Return to your roots and see what pieces of home still shape the artist you've become.

DAY 266: CREATIVITY IS NOT ABOUT CONTROL

You don't need to have it all figured out. Creativity isn't about rigid paths or perfect plans – it's about flow. What happens when you loosen your grip, when you stop forcing every detail into place? That's when the magic happens. Letting go creates space for the unexpected. Perfectionism narrows your vision, but trust in the process opens doors to ideas you couldn't have planned for. Those moments of serendipity, the happy accidents – that's where your most meaningful work often lives. When you allow things to unfold naturally, you discover freedom and creativity in its truest form. Trust your instincts and give your creativity room to breathe.

CHALLENGE

Embrace Imperfection: choose a creative project and let go of one 'perfect' detail you've been obsessing over. Allow yourself to work freely, without overthinking the outcome. What surprises emerged when you gave yourself permission to let go?

DAY 267: SAY NO MORE

Here's a wild act of creative rebellion: saying 'no'. It might seem counter-intuitive, but 'no' is one of the most powerful creative tools you have. When you say no to projects, opportunities or ideas that don't align with your vision, you make space for what truly matters. No to distractions. No to obligations that drain you. No to the ideas that pull you in directions you never wanted to go. Every 'no' is a boundary that protects your energy, your time and your art. It's a bold declaration of focus – of prioritizing what moves you forward. Saying no isn't selfish. It's clarity. It's the act of standing firm in your vision and carving out the path you were meant to walk. So today, give yourself permission to say it: no.

CHALLENGE

Today, say no to one thing that doesn't align with your vision or drains your energy – whether it's an unnecessary task, a distracting idea or an obligation you've taken on out of guilt. Use the time and energy you save to prioritize something that truly matters to you.

DAY 268: SUBCONSCIOUS MIND

Your creative mind is always at work, even in the quiet, unnoticed spaces between projects. What if you could leave yourself little signals to trigger that subconscious brilliance? A word scribbled in a notebook, an image pinned on a wall, a song that stirs something deep. These subtle cues infiltrate your creative brain, planting seeds that grow while you're not even looking. It's about trusting that creativity doesn't just happen when you're consciously trying – it's always bubbling beneath the surface. So, start leaving yourself messages. Scatter inspiration around you like breadcrumbs and let your subconscious pick them up when the time is right. Your art is brewing, even when you're not aware of it. Let the subconscious do its magic.

CHALLENGE

Grab a few note cards or scraps of paper and write down inspiring
'I am' statements, creative affirmations or ideas that spark something in you. Tape them up around your workspace, tuck them into a notebook or place them where you'll see them throughout your day. Let these little cues infiltrate your subconscious, planting seeds for your next creative breakthrough.

DAY 269: YOU ARE WHAT YOU CONSUME

Every scroll, every click, every video – it all adds up. The ideas you feed your mind, the voices you surround yourself with, the content you binge when you're tired or uninspired . . . it shapes you more than you realize. You can't expect clarity while flooding your system with noise. You can't create something original while drowning in everyone else's voice.

The truth is, you are what you consume. Not just physically, but creatively, emotionally, spiritually. Your inputs shape your outputs.

So, choose them with care. Protect your attention like your art depends on it – because it does.

CHALLENGE

Audit your inputs today. Pay close attention to what you're consuming. Identify one thing that's cluttering your mind and take a break from it. It could be social media, your favourite TV show or a negative coworker always venting to you. Then, replace it with something that inspires or grounds you.

DAY 270: BEING ALONE DOESN'T HAVE TO BE LONELY

There's a big difference between being lonely and being alone. If you're feeling stuck, unable to make clear choices or connect to your creative core, it might be time to pause and spend some time with your best friend: you. Being alone isn't isolation; it's a chance to reconnect with yourself, to hear your own voice above the constant hum of others. When you step away from the noise, you create space to think clearly, feel deeply and rediscover the parts of yourself that often get buried in the buzz. Solitude doesn't have to feel empty. It can be full of clarity, reflection and renewal. It's in these moments of quiet that you remember who you are and what truly matters to you. Alone, you can create from a place of authenticity, untangled from outside influences. Step back, not to escape, but to come home to yourself.

CHALLENGE

Spend 30 minutes alone today, free from distractions. Use this time to journal, meditate or simply sit with your thoughts. Reflect on what surfaces when you give yourself space to hear your own voice. Let this quiet moment guide your next creative step.

DAY 271: CREATIVE RITUALS

Rituals ground you. They signal to your mind and body that it's time to shift into a different space, a space where ideas can flow more freely. By setting the stage with intention, you create a sanctuary for your creativity to thrive. What small rituals do you practise before creating? Maybe it's lighting a candle, taking a deep breath or organizing your workspace just right. These little acts are more than just habits – they're gateways into your creative flow. It's not about the ritual itself, but what it represents: a moment to pause, to clear away distractions and to open yourself up to inspiration. Whether it's a simple gesture or an elaborate routine, these moments can centre you and create the ideal conditions for your best work to emerge.

CHALLENGE

Today, design a small ritual to signal the start of your creative work. It could be lighting a candle, making a cup of tea, playing a favourite song or taking a deep breath. Practise this ritual before you create, and notice how it shifts your mindset.

DAY 272: RECHARGING ISN'T A LUXURY

Creating from the heart is powerful, but it can also take a toll. Every time you pour yourself into your work, you share pieces of your emotions, your experiences and your truths. Vulnerability is what makes your art meaningful, but the emotional labour it demands is real. Recharging isn't indulgent; it's essential. Find what restores you – a walk in nature, meditation, time with people who ground you or simply a moment of stillness. Your art thrives on your vulnerability, but you can't pour from an empty well. Care for yourself as deeply as you care for your craft, so you can keep showing up with all of your heart.

CHALLENGE

Recharge with Intention: Take 15 minutes today to do something that replenishes your energy. Whether it's stepping outside, practising mindfulness or journalling, focus on giving yourself the care you need.

DAY 273: CREATIVE INTEGRITY

When you create, you're not just making something for yourself. You're speaking to someone else, and that's a responsibility. Every word, every image, every piece of work carries weight because it's your moment to say something that matters. Holding that responsibility every day can feel enormous. It's easy to get lost in the pressure, but the key is to remember who you're talking to and why you're doing this in the first place. Your audience isn't just a faceless group; they're real people who need to hear your voice, your truth. Creating with integrity means staying true to that connection. It means not cutting corners, not compromising your message for convenience or applause. It's about knowing that what you're making is meant to reach someone on the other side. Keep them in your heart as you work and let that guide you forward.

CHALLENGE

Connect with Your Audience: Take a moment to picture the person you're creating for – someone who needs your work, your message or your voice. Write them a short note as if you were speaking directly to them. What do you want them to feel, understand or take away?

DAY 274: WHY CREATIVE RESISTANCE MATTERS

There is sometimes nothing harder on this planet than the thing you know you're supposed to do. Creative resistance is real, and it's fierce. The very fact that it's so hard to push through is proof that it's worth doing. Resistance forces you to dig deeper, to commit harder, to find your voice even when the world is loud and chaotic. It's a necessary part of creating because without resistance, there's no growth. So, when the noise gets louder, when everything feels like it's going wrong, remember this: resistance isn't here to stop you. It's here to push you to the next level. Keep going, because what's on the other side is worth it.

CHALLENGE

Face the Resistance: Identify one creative task you've been avoiding because it feels too hard or frustrating. Commit to working on it for just 20 minutes today, no matter the distractions or challenges. Embrace the noise, the chaos and the resistance, and focus on making progress, not perfection.

DAY 275: GRATITUDE IN CREATIVITY

Gratitude is more than just a feeling – it's fuel for your creativity. It's easy to get caught up in the pursuit of the next idea, the next project, the next big moment. But pause for a second and think about the gift you already have: the ability to create. The act of bringing something new into the world, something that didn't exist before, is sacred. Gratitude grounds you in that truth. It reminds you to be thankful not only for the creative process but for the life that allows it. Your experiences, your struggles, your joys – these are the things that shape your art. When you're grateful for where you are and what you have, your creativity flows more freely.

CHALLENGE

Take 10 minutes to write down three things you're grateful for in your creative journey – whether it's your ability to create, a recent project or the experiences that shape your art.

DAY 276: UNPLANNED MOMENTS

The name *Create.Repeat* came to life in the shower – one of those quiet, unplanned moments when inspiration was free to strike. It's in those effortless, unguarded times – when you've let go of the pressure and expectations – that the most transformative ideas emerge. These moments aren't accidents; they're the result of giving yourself the space to be surprised. Your life needs these pauses. Build time into your day where you're not focused on *doing* but simply *being*. Walk, rest, let your mind wander without direction. Ideas come when you step away, when you let go and when you make room for the unexpected to unfold.

Sometimes, the most powerful thing you can do is create space – and watch as inspiration fills it. So, how do you cultivate this brilliance? By trusting that the greatest ideas don't come from chasing them.

CHALLENGE

Take a walk, stare out of a window or sit quietly without an agenda.
Allow your mind to wander freely, with no pressure to create.
Afterwards, jot down any ideas or insights that came to you during this pause. Trust that the space you create invites brilliance to emerge.

DAY 277: LISTEN TO DOUBT – SOMETIMES

You might be feeling doubt, but maybe it's there for a reason. This time, it's not all about insecurity. What if the doubt you're carrying is trying to tell you something important? Maybe this isn't the right thing for you. Maybe you're in the wrong job, spending each day twisted in knots, pushing through when everything inside is telling you to stop. Doubt isn't always a roadblock to overcome – it can be a signal. A nudge that something is out of alignment, that this path isn't yours to follow. And that's okay. Maybe today is the first step towards looking for other options, exploring new avenues that feel more like home. Not all creative paths are meant for you and that's where the power lies. Listening to the doubt, letting it guide you towards something that truly resonates. Maybe today, you begin to trust that voice and take the first step in a new direction.

CHALLENGE

Doubt. Instead of dismissing it, write down what it might be trying to tell you. Is something out of alignment? What might need to change? Identify one small step you can take today to explore a path that feels more true to you. Let doubt guide you towards clarity and possibility.

DAY 278: WHEN ART IS A CALLING

For some, art is just a hobby – a way to pass the time or dabble in creativity. But for others, it's more than that. It's a calling, something that runs deep, woven into the very fabric of who they are. It's not something you *choose* to do; it's something you *have* to do. *Create.Repeat* is that calling. It's a testament to the fact that when creativity runs in your DNA, you don't just make things – you answer with a deeper pull. You commit to creating with purpose and intention, even when it's difficult, even when the world feels like it's working against you. When art is your calling, it's not just about the end result. It's about the journey, the process and the belief that what you're doing matters. Honour that pull, even when it feels heavy. It's in those moments, when you keep showing up despite the challenges, that you truly honour your creative soul.

CHALLENGE

Write down what drives you – what makes art feel like a calling rather than just a pastime. Then, commit to one action today that honours that pull, whether it's starting a new project, revisiting an unfinished piece or simply creating for the sake of the process. Show up and remind yourself why this journey matters to you.

DAY 279: CREATIVITY AS A LIFELINE

There are days when everything feels like it's spiralling, when the weight of it all threatens to pull you under. But creativity, your vision, has the power to pull you out. It becomes your lifeline, reminding you of your purpose and the possibilities beyond the chaos. When life feels out of control, creating gives you a way to regain focus. It pulls you out of the spiral and into a place where you can shape your world, even if only in small ways. Vision gives you something to hold on to – an anchor in the storm, a reminder that no matter how overwhelming things get, you still have control over what you create. So, when the spiral starts, let creativity pull you back. Lean into your vision and allow it to guide you out of the noise and back to yourself. Sometimes, creating is the only way to find solid ground again.

CHALLENGE

When you feel overwhelmed, take a moment to create – write, sketch or build something simple. Let it ground you and bring clarity through the chaos.

DAY 280: CREATIVE FLOW VS. CREATIVE BLOCK

Cultivating flow is about creating the right conditions. It's not about forcing inspiration but about setting the stage for it. Routine helps – whether that's starting with a small ritual, clearing your workspace or giving yourself permission to play without pressure. Flow thrives when you let go of perfectionism and allow yourself to experiment freely. When you hit a block, don't fight it. Step back. Shift your focus. Try something different – take a walk, work on a new medium or give yourself space to breathe. Blocks are part of the process, and sometimes the best way through is to let go of the need for progress and allow your creativity to find its way back. Flow isn't always constant but with patience and the right mindset, you can find it more often – and when the block hits, trust that it's temporary.

CHALLENGE

Create the conditions for flow today. Start with a small ritual – clear your space, light a candle or play a favourite song. Then, work on a creative task without pressure, letting go of perfectionism. If you hit a block, step away and do something different. Reflect afterwards on how these shifts impacted your creative process.

DAY 281: CREATE IT UNTIL YOU MAKE IT

The phrase 'fake it until you make it' has become so ingrained in our cultural dialogue that its implications often go unquestioned. While it can serve as a temporary coping mechanism in certain situations, it also carries a detrimental message that can erode one's self-confidence.

Repeatedly telling yourself that you're 'faking it' insinuates that you're not truly deserving of your achievements or opportunities. It fosters imposter syndrome, self-doubt and feeling like a fraud. The truth is: you are not a fraud. Everything you've created in your craft is a testament to your talent, dedication and hard work. Your business, your talent, your creativity – they are all real and valid.

Banish the notion of 'faking it' and instead embrace the creative act. You are perfectly primed and ready to master it. Believe in yourself and your abilities, because you are as real and deserving as they come. Create it until you make it.

CHALLENGE

Finish the sentences and change the beliefs you hold about your creative ability:

I am not an imposter. I am _____

(i.e. a capable and competent individual who belongs in my field)

I am not a fraud. I am _____

(i.e. deserving of respect and recognition)

I am not a failure. I deserve to pursue _____

DAY 282: THE MYTH OF MAKING IT

The idea of 'making it' is the wrong goal. If you're always chasing a life that exists somewhere in the distance, you risk missing the life unfolding right in front of you. The beauty is in the process – the late nights, the sparks of inspiration, the struggle to bring an idea to life. The art itself is where the joy lives, not in some imagined future where it's all neatly tied up. Maybe one day we'll see that distant horizon as worth the chase. But for now, we're betting on the work. On the messy, imperfect, beautiful act of creating. Because today, making the art *is* making it.

CHALLENGE

Celebrate the Process: Take a moment to appreciate where you are in your creative journey. Write down one part of the process – big or small – that brings you joy.

DAY 283: THE ART OF PATIENCE IN CREATIVITY

Believe us when we say – anything worth creating is worth the wait. Creativity doesn't bend to your timeline, no matter how much you want it to. The rush is intoxicating; the need to see things done and out in the world as fast as possible. But trust us, the holdout – the patience – is never regretted. Letting your work evolve naturally, giving it the space to breathe and unfold, is part of the magic. Rushing might give you a result, but it won't give you your best work. The process of waiting, of refining, of letting your ideas simmer and grow into something more than you imagined – that's where the real power lies.

CHALLENGE

Choose a project you're working on and give it space to evolve naturally. Resist the urge to rush to the finish line. Instead, spend time refining one aspect, letting your ideas simmer and grow. Reflect on how patience impacts the quality and depth of your work. Remember, the best creations take time.

DAY 284: THE ROLE OF PLAY

The more you master your craft, the more serious things seem to get. Deadlines, expectations and the pressure to be perfect can take over. But what if the key to mastery isn't in the seriousness but in the play? When you allow yourself to experiment, to mess around with your ideas, to approach your work like a curious beginner, that's when you open new doors. Play unlocks creativity in ways that perfectionism can't. It strips away the pressure and invites you to explore freely. Mastery doesn't mean locking into a rigid process – it means knowing when to let go, when to break the rules and when to follow your instincts. Play takes your work to new heights because it invites spontaneity, new perspectives and breakthroughs that only happen when you're not afraid to take risks. So, the next time you feel yourself getting serious, remind yourself: play is where mastery truly begins.

CHALLENGE

Try something you've never done before, break your usual rules or approach your work with a beginner's mindset.

DAY 285: CREATIVE ENERGY VS. CREATIVE OUTPUT

How do you manage your creative energy? It's not just about how much you can create, but how you sustain that energy and passion over time. Burnout is real – most of us learn that the hard way. As a creative professional, this is something you'll want to understand deeply. Creative output is important, but if you constantly drain your energy without replenishing it, the well will run dry. It's about balance. What practices keep your creative spirit alive? Whether it's taking breaks, seeking inspiration in nature or finding moments of stillness, refuelling is essential. The trick isn't just to create endlessly, but to nurture your energy so that your creativity flows consistently. Protect your passion. Learn to pace yourself and create sustainable habits that keep your creative fire burning for the long haul.

CHALLENGE

Draw a simple diagram or map of your creative energy – marking what fuels you and what drains you. Be honest about the habits, activities or thoughts that impact your flow. Then, choose one energy-draining habit to reduce and one energy-boosting practice to amplify this week.

DAY 286: THE POWER OF REPETITION

Repetition often gets a bad rap, but what if it's the key to mastery? The more you do something, the better you get at it. Each time you revisit the same idea, theme or technique, you deepen your understanding, refine your skills and sharpen your creative vision. Repetition isn't about mindless repetition – it's about pushing through the familiar to find something new. It's about practising over and over, not to reach perfection, but to discover the nuances and layers you missed the first time around. Repeating doesn't just make you better – it reveals the signs hidden in the work. When you repeat, you're committing to growth. You're embracing the journey, knowing that every iteration brings you closer to mastery. So, keep going. Keep creating. Keep repeating. Because the only way to get better is to show up, again and again.

CHALLENGE

Revisit something you've made before – a sketch, a poem, a photo – and try creating a new version of it. Notice what feels easier, what's changed, and what surprises you this time around.

DAY 287: EXPRESSION

As creatives, we are sensitive souls who feel everything – the highs and the lows, the beauty and the pain. And sometimes, those lows can feel overwhelming, like a heavy weight pressing down on our spirit. Again, the opposite of depression isn't happiness. It's not about forcing joy or pretending everything is okay. The real antidote is expression. When we create, we give voice to what we feel. We take the weight inside and turn it into something tangible, something real.

Expression is our release. It's how we process, how we heal, how we make sense of the world around us. For creatives, art isn't just about making things – it's about survival. It's how we stay connected to ourselves when everything feels like it's falling apart. So, if you're in that place where the world feels heavy, don't wait for happiness to come. Create. Express what you're feeling, even if it's raw, even if it's messy. Because expression is what keeps you moving forward.

CHALLENGE

Today, channel whatever you're feeling – whether it's heavy, raw or messy – into a creative act.

DAY 288: YOU ARE WORTHY

Creativity doesn't require permission. It exists in you simply because you exist. You don't have to justify your creativity. You just have to embrace it. It's your right to make things, to put your ideas into the world, to express yourself, regardless of judgement or outcome. It's not about whether your art is perfect, whether it's praised or rejected – it's about your willingness to engage in the process. You don't need permission. You don't need validation. Worthiness doesn't come from outside. It's already within you. It's about giving yourself the freedom to create, to exist, to express without holding back. So, what does being worthy of creating mean? It means knowing that *you belong* in the act of creation – right now, as you are.

CHALLENGE

Share your 'showing up' journey publicly today – whether through a quick social post, a journal entry or a conversation with a friend. Let the act of sharing keep you accountable for continuing to show up, and observe how external accountability shifts your mindset.

DAY 289: FIND YOUR SPIELBERG MOMENT

Steven Spielberg's journey is a testament to resilience and perseverance. Rejected by the prestigious USC School of Cinematic Arts, Spielberg faced numerous setbacks early in his career. Yet, these rejections didn't deter him; they fuelled his determination. He started small, directing short films and working on television shows, honing his craft with each project.

Spielberg's breakthrough came when he directed *Jaws*, a project fraught with challenges, including technical issues and budget constraints. Instead of being overwhelmed, Spielberg embraced these obstacles, using them to push his creativity further. The result was a cinematic masterpiece that not only redefined the thriller genre but also solidified his reputation as a visionary filmmaker.

Every rejection, every failure is an opportunity to refine your skills and grow. Your 'Spielberg moment' will come not from avoiding challenges but from diving into them and using each experience to evolve. Remember, setbacks are not the end – they're the stepping stones to your own breakthrough.

CHALLENGE

Watch a Steven Spielberg film and study his craft. Pay attention to how he uses camera movement, music and performances to tell a story. Then, reflect on how you can apply that level of intentionality to your own creative work. What techniques or ideas can you learn from his approach?

DAY 290: IT'S NOT ABOUT BEING THE MOST UNIQUE

Do you question your worth when you feel like your work isn't 'original enough'? How do you overcome the pressure to be unique and still find value in your voice, even when it feels familiar? We would be lying if we said this didn't hold us back for 10 years before we started *Create.Repeat*. The constant doubt, the fear that our work wasn't different or innovative enough – those thoughts kept us stuck for far too long. But the truth is, originality doesn't always come from something entirely new. Sometimes it's about how *you* bring your own voice, your own experiences and your own perspective to the table. You see how just doing something can sometimes change your life? You really never know what will happen until you take that first step. It's not about being the most unique; it's about showing up and expressing what's true to you.

CHALLENGE

Choose a piece of work you've been hesitant to start or share because it doesn't feel 'original enough'. Begin by adding something uniquely *you* – your voice, your story or your perspective. Reflect on how your personal touch transforms the work.

DAY 291: FEELING GOOD

Creativity isn't easy – it's transformative. Picture this: 'Feeling Good' by Nina Simone plays behind you as you read these words. The boldness of the horns, the powerful rhythm – it's the sound of resilience and renewal. Simone didn't write the song, but when she recorded it in 1965, she made it her own. Her performance wasn't just music; it was a declaration of strength, a cry for equality and a testament to breaking through resistance. You, too, have a message to share. Every time you create, you're moving through your own struggles and transforming them into something meaningful. Like the way Simone holds nothing back in that final stretch – a burst of raw emotion breaking barriers – you push through the weight of the process to reach that moment of 'I'm feeling good.' Your power lies in showing up and working through the challenges.

CHALLENGE

Choose a song that resonates deeply with you, like 'Feeling Good' or another track that inspires resilience. Listen to it as you work, letting the rhythm and emotion guide your creative process.

DAY 292: PERMISSION TO DABBLE

Here's your permission to dabble! You're not just starting projects and leaving them unfinished – you're building stepping stones that shape your next ideas. You are allowed to dedicate your weekend to knitting fifteen neck scarves and never touch the needles again. That's part of being a creative. Not everything you make needs to be monumental or life changing. Your creative worth isn't defined by how long you stick with something or how impactful it seems. The value lies in the exploration, in the freedom to create, express and move on. Every experiment, every attempt, is part of the journey. What you're looking for will reveal itself as you keep going, one step at a time.

CHALLENGE

Choose a new or unfinished creative project and work on it for 20 minutes today. When the time is up, leave it behind without any pressure to return to it. Focus on the joy of trying, experimenting and moving forward. Reflect: what did this process spark for your next idea?

DAY 293: BEAUTY IN EXPRESSION

There's something so beautiful about watching people express themselves and be happy. It doesn't really matter if it's 'good'. Isn't all art subjective, anyway? Beauty is in the eye of the beholder, right? Some of these passages will hit you like a ton of bricks. Others might feel like they pass by unnoticed. That's life. We all see and hear what we need to at different moments, and everything we create goes through thousands of personal filters before we decide what resonates. You see how that should give you *freedom* instead of pressure? If you're happy, keep going. Art doesn't have to be tied to success. Expression is about joy, about feeling alive in the moment. Let that be enough.

CHALLENGE

Take a moment to reflect on what you find beautiful – whether it's a sound, a colour, a memory or a feeling. Infuse that into your work today if you can.

DAY 294: LIFE AND DEATH

Creation is a cycle – something comes to life, exists for a time and eventually transforms, fades or leaves a space behind. This isn't just the nature of art; it's the nature of life. The work we create carries meaning in its presence, but its absence carries meaning too. In those spaces where something once was, a new kind of energy exists – a memory, a shift, a mark left on the world. Creation and absence aren't opposites; they're partners in a constant exchange. As creatives, we live in this rhythm, choosing what to bring forth, what to let go and how to navigate the quiet moments between.

CHALLENGE

Today, if you find yourself in that in-between, honour it. Reflect on what was, and let it guide you towards what's next. Absence doesn't mean the end; it means there's room for something new to emerge. What will you create in this space?

DAY 295: TENSION BETWEEN FREEDOM AND STRUCTURE

How does complete creative freedom impact your process? It's something we crave, but too much freedom can be paralyzing. When there are no boundaries, no guidelines, sometimes you end up floating, unsure where to land. That's why, for some of us, a 9-to-5 job feels suffocating – like you're boxed in, following someone else's rules. But then, full-time freelancing can feel wild, unhinged, with no clear direction. The truth is, we need both. Structure gives us a foundation, a framework to push against, while freedom lets us explore and expand. The magic happens when you balance the two – when you find flexibility within structure, allowing your ideas to flow but giving them enough form to take shape. It's about creating your own rules and then breaking them when you need to. In the end, neither complete freedom nor rigid structure is the answer. It's the tension between them that unlocks your best ideas.

CHALLENGE

Set three clear boundaries – like a time limit, a specific medium or a theme – and then allow yourself total freedom within those limits.

DAY 296: CREATING UNDER CONSTRAINTS

How do limits – whether time, resources or external conditions – affect your creativity? As frustrating as they can be, boundaries often push you to think in new, innovative ways. When you don't have all the tools or materials you imagined, what do you do? You get creative.

As creatives, we need to work with what we have. The absence of endless resources doesn't stop the work from happening – it's what makes the work better. Constraints force you to think smarter, to push beyond what you thought was possible. They create opportunities for fresh ideas, for surprising solutions that might never have emerged in perfect conditions.

Don't let limitations stop you. Instead, let them challenge and inspire you. Some of the most powerful work comes from the struggle of creating under constraints.

CHALLENGE

Identify the biggest challenge or obstacle in your creative process today. Instead of letting it hold you back, find a way to use it as inspiration or a unique limitation to work within. Let it guide you towards a fresh perspective or unexpected solution. See what happens when you turn the problem into part of the process.

DAY 297: MAKE A MOVE

What is your message? Ours is simple: you can do whatever you want to do. You can create, dream, build and construct anything from nothing. From this place of inspiration, we hope you take action and do the things you want in this one lifetime. You get one life. Let that hit you today. Are you living the life you want? Are you working on projects that make you feel alive? Are you in a job you love? Are you doing the damn thing? If not, today is the first step towards that life.

CHALLENGE

Slam this book down and make a move.

DAY 298: RESPECT THE CLOCK

Sure, time moves in a straight line – but creativity doesn't run on a clock. Deadlines loom, schedules demand progress and projects need finishing. So how do you navigate time without letting it dictate your creativity? It's a balance of structure and surrender. Some thrive under pressure, finding energy in the ticking clock. Others need space to let ideas simmer and evolve. Neither is right or wrong – it's about knowing how you work best and leaning into that rhythm.

Time shapes creativity, but it doesn't have to control it. When you stop fighting against the clock and start working with it, creativity becomes less of a race and more of a flow. Find your rhythm, honour the process and trust that your best work will come when you're fully present in both the push and the pause.

CHALLENGE

Reflect on how you engage with time in your creative process. Set aside two focused blocks today – one where you work under a time constraint (like 30 minutes to complete a task) and another where you allow yourself to create without a set endpoint.

DAY 299: LET ART HEAL YOU

Today, let art heal you. How can creativity help you process the difficult emotions – grief, anger, loneliness – that feel too heavy to carry? Art has a way of turning what feels impossible into something tangible, something you can see, hear or touch. It gives form to the feelings that words can't capture. When life feels overwhelming, making art can help you make sense of the emotional complexities. Creativity becomes your compass, showing you that while you may not have control over the emotions, you can shape them into something meaningful. Your art should be a space for healing, for understanding and for finding peace in the midst of chaos.

CHALLENGE

Take 15 minutes today to create something that expresses a difficult emotion you're feeling – whether it's through writing, drawing, music or another medium. Don't worry about how it looks or sounds; focus on letting the emotion flow through the act of creating. When you're done, take a moment to reflect on how the process shifted your perspective or lightened the weight.

DAY 300: THE BEAUTY OF CHANGE

Life, friends, creativity – it's all constantly in motion. If we embraced this truth more often, maybe we'd create more, heal faster and hurt less. Nothing stays exactly as it is, and that's not a flaw – it's the essence of life itself.

When we stop resisting change and accept that things evolve, we free ourselves from unnecessary weight. It's not about holding on too tightly; it's about appreciating each phase as it comes, knowing that every shift brings new possibilities. Doesn't that make everything feel a little lighter? The beauty is in the movement, the transformation and the ever-changing flow of life.

CHALLENGE

Reflect on a recent change in your life – big or small. Create something that represents this transformation, whether it's a sketch, a poem, a playlist or even a mood board. Let the process help you appreciate the beauty in how things evolve and the possibilities that come with it.

DAY 301: NOTHING CHANGES
IF NOTHING CHANGES

So, you want change? Then it's time to act. What are you willing to do to bring about that change? It begins with cultivating new habits, stepping outside of your comfort zone and embracing unfamiliar surroundings. But perhaps most importantly, it requires a shift in your inner dialogue with yourself. Replace self-doubt with self-belief, fear with courage and complacency with ambition. Challenge the status quo, push the boundaries of your creativity and dare to dream beyond the confines of what is known. Embrace the chaos, experiment with new forms and watch as your creative work and horizons transform in the most exciting of ways.

CHALLENGE

Change up your routine:
- Go create somewhere else today.
- Try using a different medium, i.e. instead of using your computer, try creating manually.
- Reconnect with the very first work of art that ever inspired you.
- Call someone who's a positive influence on your life and thank them.
- Have something different for lunch.

DAY 302: THE POWER OF SILENCE

How does silence inform your work? In a world where we're constantly checking in on every human in our lives – while trying to complete something – you lose focus. You lose yourself. There comes a time when you need to focus on you and your work. Silence, introspection, solitude – these are the tools that unlock ideas more than noise and busyness ever will. In the quiet, you hear things you couldn't before. It's where your deepest ideas surface, where creativity isn't clouded by distraction. These moments of stillness allow you to see clearly, to connect with what's inside of you, rather than constantly reacting to the outside world. Silence isn't empty. It's full of potential, waiting for you to listen.

CHALLENGE

Spend 30 minutes today in complete silence. Turn off your phone, step away from distractions and sit with your thoughts. Use this time to reflect, brainstorm or simply let your mind wander. When the silence ends, capture one idea, insight or feeling that emerged during this stillness, and let it guide your next creative step.

DAY 303: GET CLEAR

What's the difference between you and them? It's clear vision. That's the defining factor – the thing that separates those who make their mark from those who struggle to find their way. Look at Steve Jobs. His genius wasn't just in his pursuit of innovation, but in his unshakeable clarity of vision. He knew exactly where he was going, and nothing could distract him from that path. Today is the day to get as clear as ever. Do you know where you're headed? Are you pursuing your creative goals with relentless focus or are you getting lost in distractions? The more clearly you see your destination, the more unstoppable you become. You have the power to bring your vision to life. But first, you have to know exactly what that vision is.

CHALLENGE

Write down your top creative goal in one clear, concise sentence. Then, list three specific actions you can take this week to move closer to that goal. Post this list somewhere you'll see it daily to keep your vision front and centre.

DAY 304: STAY TRUE

Stay true to your art. Refuse to be boxed in by others' expectations, labels or ideas of what you should create. You're here to express your vision, and that means standing firm in what feels right to you – never compromising the core of your work just to fit into a mould. But here's the nuance: sometimes, things aren't working. Sometimes, the shift isn't about giving up your vision – it's about adapting, evolving and finding the path that best serves your art. There's no shame in changing direction when it's needed. Just remember, the change comes from you – not from external pressures. Let your creativity flow freely, without fear of confinement, and when the time comes, make those shifts from a place of strength, not compromise.

CHALLENGE

Reflect on your current creative project. Ask yourself: is this true to my vision or have I let outside expectations shape it? If it feels authentic, take one step today to deepen that alignment. If it feels off, identify one small shift you can make to bring it closer to your original intention. Document your decision and how it impacts your process.

DAY 305: YOUR RELATIONSHIP TO FAILURE

Failure is like relationships – there are all different kinds. Some are short-lived, barely leaving a mark. Others stay with you, teaching you something profound. Some failures feel like heartbreak, while others simply fizzle out, barely making a dent in your life. And just like with relationships, you don't always know where they're going to lead. Not every failure will be the end of the world. Some will be minor, some will shift your entire path, and some might even lead you to the place you're meant to be. Failure has layers, just like relationships. It's not something to fear – it's something to understand and grow from. Your fear has made failure feel too big, but just like in relationships, there's always something to learn, something to gain and something to help you move forward.

CHALLENGE

Reflect on a recent failure and write a 'letter' to it, as if it were a person you had a relationship with. What did it teach you? How did it impact your journey? Be honest about how it felt but also acknowledge the growth it brought. When you're done, use those insights to inform your next step forward.

DAY 306: BE WEIRD FOR YOU FIRST

Experiment. Be weird. Push what's normal. Maybe that's where the thing is. Maybe that's where your freedom lies. Do it for you first – find the pulse, the rhythm that makes your heart beat faster. Maybe others need to see it, maybe they don't. But always, always be weird for you first. That's the kid inside of you, still creating with their heart, not their head. The one who didn't care what people thought, who just made things because it felt right. That's where the magic is – before the world told you how to create, before you learned to fit in. So, get weird. Be bold. And let that part of you take the lead.

CHALLENGE

Create something today that feels completely 'weird' to you – something unconventional, silly or outside your usual style. Don't worry about sharing it or perfecting it; just let yourself play. Afterwards, reflect on how it felt to create without any expectations or judgement.

DAY 307: LOVE THE PROCESS

The bottom line is, you have to love the process. The creation is what you'll spend your life doing. Your entire life won't be standing in an art gallery saying, 'Wow, look what I made.' No, your life will be in the making of it. If you're feeling burned out – tired of sculpting, painting, going to the studio every day – it's time to take a moment and reflect. Do you still love the parts of doing what you love? The day you hate learning the sheet music, maybe playing in the orchestra isn't where your heart is anymore. Find the thing you can love doing every day. The performance is only 1% of it. The living happens in the process. So, find the work that makes you feel alive in the doing, not just in the applause.

CHALLENGE

Spend today focusing on one small part of your creative process that you usually overlook or rush through. Whether it's mixing colours, tuning your instrument or brainstorming ideas, approach it with care and appreciation. Reflect on what you enjoy about this step and how it contributes to the bigger picture of your work.

DAY 308: DECIDE

Decide who you want to be. You know those people – the ones who wear clogs and baggy dresses like it's a second skin? At some point, they made a choice. They decided, *This is who I am,* and then they owned it. You have the same power, the same set of choices in front of you. It's time to pick a lane and go down it for a while. Who do you want to present yourself as? What version of yourself do you want the world to see? It's not about getting it perfect but about making a choice and committing to it. So, who's it going to be? The world is waiting for your answer.

CHALLENGE

Write down three words that describe the version of yourself you want to embody. Then, take one tangible action today that aligns with those words – whether it's how you dress, how you work or how you communicate. Step into that identity and own it.

DAY 309: CREATIVE CHRISTMAS

The holidays – why do they feel so heavy for creatives? Maybe it's because this time of year brings up feelings of expectation, reflection and comparison. We're sensitive souls, tuned into the nuances of everything, and during the holidays that sensitivity heightens. It's not just about the gifts or gatherings – it's about who you are, what you've accomplished and how you fit into the world. For creatives, it can feel like the world is asking for something big, something grand, but creativity doesn't always work on a holiday schedule. Sometimes the pressure to create or be 'on' during this time of celebration feels suffocating. But here's the truth: you don't have to create anything extra, you don't have to be more than you are. It's okay to step back, to reflect and to let yourself just *be*. Give yourself the same grace you offer others, and let the holidays unfold as they will – without the weight of expectation on your shoulders.

CHALLENGE

Take 30 minutes today to create something purely for yourself – something with no audience, no purpose and no expectation. It could be a doodle, a poem or a melody. Let it be a gift to yourself, a reminder that creativity can exist without pressure or performance.

DAY 310: TELL THEM

Maybe as creatives, it's time we start using our art to tell them how. Tell them how to treat us, where we're going, what we stand for. Your art is more than just expression – it's a declaration. A way to state your intentions to the world. This might seem far-fetched, but art has always been how we communicate with the world. It's how we shape the conversation, how we influence, how we push forward. We have that power. So why not wield it? Why not use your creativity to set the record straight, to tell them exactly what they need to know about who you are and where you're headed? Take the power. Tell them.

CHALLENGE

Create something today that communicates a clear message about who you are or what you stand for. It could be a statement piece, a bold design or even a simple phrase written in your own style. Share it with the world or keep it for yourself, but make sure it tells your story unmistakably.

DAY 311: PUSH PAST

Today, push past what you think is good. You have the power to train your brain, to expand your creativity beyond what feels comfortable or safe. What you think is 'good' right now might just be the beginning. There's more inside of you – more ideas, more expression waiting to break through – if you're willing to push beyond the surface. Your brain can stretch, it can grow, it can take on new challenges. Don't settle for what feels good enough. Expand your capacity, push the boundaries and see what new heights you can reach.

CHALLENGE

Take a project you feel is 'good enough' and spend an extra 30 minutes on it today. Experiment with one bold idea or unexpected element that stretches your comfort zone. Reflect on how this additional effort transforms the work and your perception of its potential.

DAY 312: IMAGINE NEW BOUNDARIES

Breaking boundaries in creativity isn't just about following the rules – it's about rewriting them. It's about imagining worlds that challenge the status quo, daring to explore what human potential could look like if we let go of society's limits. As creators, you have the power to shape not just stories, but possibilities. What would the future look like if it were shaped by your vision? What radical changes could you inspire in others? Creativity is not confined to what already exists – it's about expanding the horizon of what could be. Don't just reflect the world – reshape it. Dream beyond the boundaries, and let your work be the force that disrupts, challenges and redefines.

CHALLENGE

Write down one rule, norm or assumption in your creative field or society that feels limiting. Then, brainstorm one bold way to challenge or rewrite it through your art. Use today to sketch, write or plan a concept that pushes past that boundary and envisions something entirely new.

DAY 313: RECOGNIZE YOUR GROWTH

There's growth. You can start to see it, bit by bit. You're showing up and with every step, you're becoming more than just someone moving from point A to B. Isn't that the point? Growth isn't always loud or dramatic. Sometimes, it's quiet. It's in the way you keep going, even when no one's watching. It's in the tiny moments where you push yourself a little harder, think a little deeper and create with a little more heart. You are becoming something more and that's what matters. Keep showing up and you'll see that growth unfold in ways you never expected.

CHALLENGE

Take 10 minutes today to reflect on your journey over the past year. Write down three specific ways you've grown as a creative – big or small. Keep this list somewhere visible as a reminder of how far you've come, and let it fuel your confidence to keep moving forward.

DAY 314: BEHIND THE SCENES

Maybe the conditions of your life are exactly what you can handle. Maybe it's best to be the kind of artist who works behind the scenes, creating without the spotlight, while still holding on to your privacy. There's power in that, too. Not every creative journey has to be public, loud or in full view of the world. Behind the scenes, you can create without pressure. You can explore, evolve and push your work without the constant gaze of others. There's freedom in that privacy – a space where you get to keep your personal life separate while still making an impact. Sometimes, staying behind the scenes means you're in control of your art and your life, and maybe that's exactly where you're meant to be.

CHALLENGE

Spend today working on a project that's just for you – something you don't plan to share with anyone else. Use this private space to experiment, explore and create without any external expectations. Reflect on how it feels to create purely for yourself and the freedom it brings to your process.

DAY 315: TIRED OF SEEING NOTHING

You're tired. Tired of creating, repeating and seeing nothing. Seeing nothing – how interesting. Maybe you're looking at the wrong thing. There's no way to be this far into the process and feel like nothing is shifting. It's not about what your literal eyes can see. The changes, the growth, the evolution – it's all happening, but it's for your soul, not for the surface. The deepest shifts often happen where no one else can see them, and sometimes even you can't. But trust that every step, every creative act, is moving you forward. You're building something. You're growing. Just because you can't see it yet doesn't mean it's not real.

CHALLENGE

Take 15 minutes to write a list of the unseen ways you've grown or shifted in your creative journey – things that may not be immediately visible to others. Reflect on how these internal changes have shaped your process, and let this list remind you that progress isn't always about what's on the surface.

DAY 316: SEEING SHADOWS

Shadows are fascinating, aren't they? They're the existence of something without the proof. You can't touch them, but you can see them. Shadows remind us that just because something isn't tangible doesn't mean it's not real. In your creative journey, think of the shadows you've been chasing – the ideas that linger just out of reach, the progress that feels invisible but is still there. Seeing shadows is acknowledging that something is taking shape, even if you can't fully grasp it yet. Trust in what's forming. Sometimes, the shadows are all the proof you need that something is coming to life.

CHALLENGE

Identify one 'shadow' in your creative process – an idea, a feeling or a piece of progress that feels intangible or just out of reach. Spend time today bringing it closer to reality. Sketch it out, write about it or take one small action towards making it tangible. Trust in its potential and let it guide your next step.

DAY 317: INTUITION

Try to understand that you're a part of something so much bigger today. You're existing in this time, in this body, with these talents, for a reason. Perhaps your creativity is tied to something ancient, something carried with you across lifetimes. Lean into that feeling, and trust that you're meant to create exactly what you're working on now. You're connected to it in ways you might not fully understand yet. Maybe your future self is trying to send you messages right now that will help you along this path. Be open. Be curious. You have nothing to lose.

CHALLENGE

Spend 10 minutes in quiet reflection or meditation today. Focus on your current creative project and let your intuition guide you. Write down any thoughts, feelings or ideas that come to mind, even if they don't seem logical or clear. Use these insights as inspiration to move forward with trust and curiosity.

DAY 318: MAKING NEW DECISIONS

Why were we always told to pick something as kids? We had to choose our favourite things and go in that direction. But maybe there's something to that – maybe as adults, we need to be given that choice again and again. As more information comes to us through this lived experience, we need to make new decisions based on that evidence. Based on everything you've lived through since your childhood, your choice might be different today, and that's 100% necessary. The truth is, you're allowed to change. You're supposed to. The artist you are today deserves to be shaped by everything you've learned along the way.

CHALLENGE

Reflect on who you are as a creative today. Write down three new decisions you'd make about your creative identity, priorities or direction based on what you've learned since you started. Choose one of these decisions and take a small step today to bring it to life.

DAY 319: TAKE NOTE

Take note. Take note of everything you need and, maybe more importantly, what you don't. Become hyperaware of the distractions – things,
habits and, maybe the hardest part, the people who no longer serve
you. That might feel ruthless but it isn't. Who and what are holding
you back? Who are the vampires sucking the energy, the air, out of
every opportunity you have and will have? You only get one life. Are
you letting someone else take up space in your creative journey that's
meant for you? It's time to recognize where your focus should be. Let
go of what drains you and make space for what helps you grow.

CHALLENGE

Make a list of three things, habits or people that drain your energy and
three that energize and inspire you. Commit to reducing one drain and
doubling down on one source of inspiration this week. Notice how this
shift impacts your focus and creativity.

DAY 320: AIM HIGHER

The people you aspire to become – the heroes, the celebrities, the idols – they're just people. Aim higher than them. By the time you reach where you're supposed to be, you'll realize that those you once put on a pedestal are just human, just like you. Be better. Aim for the stars, and don't limit yourself by thinking you can only reach as far as they did. Be the best version of *you*, and that will make you the only one. Your path isn't theirs. It's yours, and it's meant to take you places beyond what you can see right now.

CHALLENGE

Write down the name of someone you admire and why you look up to them. Then, list three ways you can go beyond their achievements in your own unique way. Take one action today that aligns with your path, aiming higher than you thought possible.

DAY 321: BE THE PERSON YOU WISH YOU HAD

This is simple and sweet. Always aim to be the person you wish you had on set, at work or in life. Being a good person – that's one simple thing that makes the creative process lighter and more joyful. When you bring light, positivity and kindness into a room, you make art fun. You create an environment where people can thrive, where the process feels like play instead of pressure. Be that person. Share your light. It's what makes the journey, and the work, truly worthwhile.

CHALLENGE

Think of a moment when you felt supported or inspired by someone. Today, channel that energy and be that person for someone else. Whether it's offering encouragement, lending a helping hand or simply showing kindness, take one action that brings light to someone's creative journey.

DAY 322: WHERE YOUR ATTENTION GOES YOUR ENERGY FLOWS

Where your attention goes, your energy flows. For creatives, it's time to wake up to that truth. Your attention is powerful – it has the ability to shape your art, your process and your life. The work you choose to pour yourself into, the thoughts you dwell on, the projects you pursue – these are where your energy flows. So, choose carefully. Invest your attention in the things that light you up, that drive you forward, that make you feel alive. Understand this power, and you'll realize you're capable of much more than you thought. Your energy is a force and where you direct it will define what you create.

CHALLENGE

Take a moment to reflect on where your attention has been focused lately. Write down three things that have been consuming your energy. Then, identify one area or project that truly excites you and shift your focus there today. Observe how redirecting your attention impacts your creativity and motivation.

DAY 323: OVERCOME THE TEST

Life has a way of sending the same wave your way, over and over, until you learn to rise above it. These challenges don't disappear until you understand why you keep bumping up against them. The lesson is part of the process – you don't get to move forward without it. Think of the ocean: the waves don't change just for you. They keep coming with the same force, again and again. You have a choice – sink or learn to surf. Face these challenges, grow with them and show yourself that you can ride any wave. This is your moment. Step up and let the tests prove just how strong you can be.

CHALLENGE

Identify one recurring challenge in your creative process or life. Take 10 minutes to reflect on what it might be trying to teach you. Write down one actionable step you can take to face it differently this time. Commit to rising above it and using the lesson to move forward.

DAY 324: BATTLE YOUR IMPOSTER

Creativity and self-doubt go hand in hand. When your work is an extension of you, it's natural to question it. But part of the journey is learning to be okay with that – embracing the vulnerability of putting yourself out there and letting people truly see you. As the initial burst of inspiration fades, doubt can become pervasive, tempting you to give up or look for excitement elsewhere. That's when the battle begins, with flow and creative abundance awaiting its victors.

CHALLENGE

- Reconnect with Your 'Knowing': This is your WHY. It's about recognizing your calling and understanding the reason you were put on this Earth. When doubt and sadness creep in, it's essential to hold on to this sense of purpose and not allow it to overshadow or consume you.
- Break It Down: Break the project down into smaller, more manageable steps. Focusing on one step at a time can make the overall process feel less overwhelming and help build momentum, reducing feelings of doubt and uncertainty.
- Engage in Creative Exploration: Take breaks from your main project to engage in creative exploration or experimentation. Trying new techniques, mediums or approaches can spark fresh ideas and perspectives, helping to counteract feelings of stagnation and doubt.
- Practise Mindfulness and Self-Care: We understand that there are simply days when your mental state needs a break. Listen to yourself. There will be times when you need to scale back and prioritize self-care. Remember, a well-rested you is an even better artist.

DAY 325: MISDIRECTED ENERGY

Are you going 100 miles per hour in the wrong direction? It's easy to throw everything you've got into a path that doesn't actually lead you where you want to go. But recognizing that mid-journey is powerful. It's never too late to stop, reassess and reroute. Ask yourself: are you moving towards your purpose or are you just moving? There's strength in slowing down, in pausing to redirect your energy to a truer path. When you course-correct, even if it feels like starting over, you're choosing clarity over speed. That's when you know you're headed somewhere real.

CHALLENGE

Take 15 minutes to assess your current creative projects or goals. Ask yourself: are these truly aligned with where I want to go or am I just staying busy? Write down one specific adjustment you can make today to redirect your energy towards a path that feels more purposeful. Then, take the first step.

DAY 326: DO YOU TRUST YOURSELF

Do you trust yourself? Really trust yourself? Self-belief is one thing, but self-trust runs deep. Could it be that the one thing holding you back is your own lack of trust in yourself? Do you trust that when met with opportunity, you'll rise to the occasion? That you have what it takes, that you deserve the chance to shine? Do you trust that when you get there, you won't sabotage your own success? Belief is powerful, but trust? That's your foundation. Trust in yourself to show up, to stay steady and to keep going when the stakes are high. Because when you do, there's nothing you can't achieve.

CHALLENGE

Write a letter to yourself, highlighting the reasons you can trust yourself – your past successes, your resilience, and your ability to rise to challenges. Keep it as a reminder for moments of doubt. Today, take one action that demonstrates that trust, whether it's committing to a project, saying yes to an opportunity or simply taking a bold step forward.

DAY 327: MEISNER TECHNIQUE FOR LIFE

Meisner taught actors to live truthfully in each moment, reacting naturally within imaginary circumstances. In life, this lesson is just as powerful. Creativity thrives on openness and adaptability – taking each moment as it is, without the weight of rigid plans or overthinking. Sometimes we pre-plan too much, trying to control every outcome. But when you stay open, each idea flows into the next, effortlessly. Let the art come to you; let life surprise you. Trust that there's something magical in simply responding to the moment as it unfolds.

CHALLENGE

Practise living truthfully in the moment today. Choose a creative exercise where you respond spontaneously – like freewriting, sketching or improvising – without overthinking or planning. Let your instincts guide you and reflect afterwards on how it felt to create in the flow of the present moment.

DAY 328: MOVEMENT AND SPACE

Some days, creativity isn't all up to you. Movement and space – what's around you – have their own way of shaping the process. Breathe in everything around you. Feel the air, the light, the subtle energy of your space. Notice how it affects you. Creation is rarely isolated from the world. It's a response to your surroundings, a dance with the space you're in. Move around, shift perspectives, try creating in a different room or outside. Feel the rhythm of where you are. Some days, the environment plays as much of a role as your own imagination. Let it shape what you make.

CHALLENGE

Change your creative environment today. Work in a new space – outside, in a different room, or even just rearranging your usual setup. Pay attention to how the change in movement and surroundings influences your process, and let it inspire something unexpected in your work.

DAY 329: THE COST OF BEING LATE

If you're late in one area, it bleeds into others. Don't mistake being late as just 'one of those things' – most times, lateness is a choice, not an accident. Sure, surprises happen, but more often, running behind sends a message to your subconscious that you don't value your commitments. Lateness is more than a lack of respect for others; it's a lack of respect for yourself. Being on time is about showing up for yourself, reinforcing your own standards. What message do you want to send? Start honouring your time and notice how everything else in your life starts to feel aligned.

CHALLENGE

Identify one area where you've been consistently 'late' – whether it's meeting deadlines, starting projects or showing up for yourself. Today, set a specific time to begin or complete something important, and stick to it. Notice how meeting this commitment impacts your sense of self-respect and alignment.

DAY 330: MOURNING THE END

Coming to the end of a project is strange – especially one that has poured so much life into you. There's this tug-of-war inside, a resistance to wrapping it up because a part of you isn't ready to let it go. This is how you know you loved the process. It wasn't just the final product you cared about, it was the journey itself. You find yourself holding on, trying to slow down, just to savour each last piece. But the beauty of endings is the mark they leave on us. This project lives in you now. Carry it forward and let its energy move you into what's next. You got this.

CHALLENGE

Take time today to reflect on a project you've recently completed or are about to finish. Write down three ways it has impacted you – what you learned, how you grew and what it gave you. Then, identify one way to honour the project as you transition into your next creative chapter.

DAY 331: COMPASSION IN CREATIVITY

Creativity and compassion go hand in hand. To create authentically, we need to be kind – to ourselves, to our process and to those around us. Sometimes, the work feels messy or imperfect; sometimes, we get stuck. But instead of criticizing, what if we learned to embrace it all with compassion? Practise speaking to yourself with the same encouragement you'd give a friend. Be gentle with your own journey. Accept that your art, just like you, will have highs and lows. And extend this empathy outward: celebrate others, support their progress and be generous with feedback. Compassion is a powerful creative force – it opens doors, builds trust and inspires more authentic work.

CHALLENGE

Write a compassionate note to yourself about where you are in your creative journey. Acknowledge your efforts, your progress and the challenges you've faced with kindness. Then, extend that compassion outward by reaching out to another creative – offer them encouragement, celebrate their work or share something that inspires them.

DAY 332: FOCUS ON WHAT YOU ARE

Stop spending energy on what you're not. You just spent all day tearing yourself down – congrats, but where did it get you? Instead, look at what you have, at the things you're good at. Shift your attention to the parts of you that are already enough. What if today, you decided to put the spotlight on your strengths? Just for a moment, let yourself believe you're exactly where you need to be. Your journey doesn't move forward by focusing on what you lack. It moves when you stand firmly in what you are. You're good at something. Start there.

CHALLENGE

List three things you're good at – skills, traits or strengths that make you unique. Pick one of them and dedicate 15 minutes today to celebrating or using it. Whether it's practising a skill, sharing it with others or reflecting on its value, focus on what makes you enough right now.

DAY 333: ALIGNMENT

When you see a moment of alignment, grab it. Today, the focus is balance – bringing together your skills, your ambitions and the parts of you that make it all possible. It's a reminder that everything you need to keep moving forward is already in you. This is a green light to push into your creativity, to build on your strengths and to find that steady rhythm in your work and life. So, take a moment to acknowledge your progress, set your sights on what's next and know that each small step builds into something powerful. Balance, create, grow – this is the momentum you're meant to build on.

CHALLENGE

Take 10 minutes today to reflect on an area of your life or work where you feel aligned – where your skills, passions and efforts come together seamlessly. Write down one action you can take to deepen that alignment and build on it. Then, take that step and feel the momentum grow.

DAY 334: ALMOST THERE

As you near the finish line, pride starts to creep in – and it should. But don't let that pride turn into complacency. This is the moment to channel every ounce of your energy, to dig deeper and to bring your absolute best to the table. You're so close, but the difference between good and great is in that final push. Don't settle for a version that falls short of your true potential. Finishing is satisfying, but finishing strong is transformative. Prove to yourself what you're capable of when you give it everything you've got. Push through, rise higher and show the world – and yourself – just how unstoppable you are.

CHALLENGE

Identify a project or task that's near completion. Instead of rushing to the finish, take time to refine and elevate it. Ask yourself: *Is this my best work?* Push yourself to go the extra mile and end with excellence. Notice how it feels to truly finish strong.

DAY 335: FORGIVE

Practising self-compassion is an act of self-love, and self-love isn't reserved for one type of person – it's for all of us. As creatives, we are vessels, channels for ideas and inspiration. Holding ourselves hostage to past mistakes or missed marks only limits what we can create next. Forgiving yourself isn't about letting things slide; it's about setting yourself free. So today, choose self-forgiveness. Embrace the truth that you are allowed to make mistakes, to grow, to evolve. Let go and give yourself permission to move forward with love for who you are right now, not just for who you're trying to become. Imagine the art you could create in a space filled with self-love and acceptance. That's the freedom we all need to reach our fullest potential.

CHALLENGE

Write down one thing you've been holding against yourself – whether it's a mistake, a missed opportunity or a moment of doubt. Then, write a forgiveness statement, releasing yourself from that weight. Keep it as a reminder that self-forgiveness is a step towards freedom and creativity. Use this energy to move forward and create with love and acceptance.

DAY 336: WORK THE MOMENT

When it's working, lean into it – work it for all it's worth. No job, project or creative flow lasts forever in its exact form, and sometimes, things change before we're ready. But while it's here, give it everything. Your current job might not always be a job; your inspiration may shift direction. So, maximize this moment, wring out every lesson, every connection, every ounce of creative energy you can. Because when it's working, it's building you up, preparing you for whatever's next. Nothing is permanent, but everything is progress. So, work it while it's working, knowing that each step forward, each creation, is taking you exactly where you need to go.

CHALLENGE

Identify one area in your life or creative work where things are currently 'working'. Spend an extra hour today fully focused on that – whether it's finishing a project, deepening a connection or pushing your inspiration further. Reflect on what you're gaining from this moment and how it's preparing you for what's next.

DAY 337: HARD TRUTHS

Other people's truths, their honesty – it's not yours to hold. Sometimes, the honesty of others can feel heavy, and it can create that strange bubble of awkward energy. But remember, their truths are theirs, not yours. You don't have to carry their honesty or the discomfort that comes with it. Instead, let it exist without absorbing it. Hold space if you need to, but don't let it weigh you down or intrude on your own creative flow. Your mind and energy are precious, meant to serve your art, your growth and your own truth. Release the weight and keep moving freely.

CHALLENGE

Think of a recent moment when someone else's truth or energy felt heavy on you. Take 10 minutes to journal about how it affected you and what you can release. Then, practise letting go by redirecting your focus to something that energizes or inspires you – whether it's a quick creative exercise or simply a moment of stillness.

DAY 338: EASY STREET

Making things look easy – it's both a blessing and a curse. There's pride in flowing through your work with grace, in creating something that feels effortless to the outside world. But here's the catch: when you make it look easy, people often forget the effort it took to get there. The hours, the mistakes, the resilience hidden beneath the polish. Remember, it's okay if not everyone sees the grit behind the grace. Your ease in creating is the result of dedication, practice and commitment. So, wear it proudly, but know that the 'effortless' look is a mark of mastery, not magic. Let it be your quiet victory, knowing that the journey is what makes the ease possible.

CHALLENGE

Reflect on a skill or creative process you've mastered to the point where it feels 'effortless'. Take 15 minutes to write about the journey it took to get there – the struggles, the growth and the persistence. Share this story with someone who might benefit from understanding the work behind the ease or keep it as a reminder of how far you've come.

DAY 339: RELENTLESS GRIND

Here is the fun reminder that this work is relentless. The truth is, this work doesn't get easier – it only asks more from you. Every level brings new challenges, new demands and, sometimes, new doubts. The old saying 'more money, more problems' rings true here. Each step forward expands the pressure, the expectations and the stakes.

The deadlines don't stop; the hustle doesn't slow. But that's where the passion comes in. This path isn't about reaching an end; it's about building a life that revolves around what you love, even on the hardest days. The relentlessness? It's proof of how deeply you're invested. You're in it because you have no other choice but to create, repeat and evolve. And though it's not easy, it's where you're meant to be.

CHALLENGE

Identify one part of your creative grind that feels particularly relentless right now. Instead of resisting it, lean into it – commit an extra 30 minutes today to that task with intention and focus. Reflect afterwards on how embracing the grind, rather than fighting it, shifts your mindset and strengthens your passion for the work.

DAY 340: STAY SWEET

There's something achingly beautiful about the sensitive soul – the artist's heart that feels everything so deeply. In a world that often demands toughness, your softness is a quiet act of rebellion. You, who sees beauty in the overlooked, who feels the weight of the smallest moments, are a reminder of what's real and what's worth protecting. Your soul deserves to be watered, nurtured and cared for. This tenderness within you is necessary, a vital balance to a world always on the edge of hardening. So, stay soft, stay sweet, stay open. Your sensitivity is a gift, both to yourself and to the world that so desperately needs it. Your gentleness is your strength.

CHALLENGE

Take a moment today to nurture your sensitive side. Write, sketch or create something inspired by a small, beautiful moment you noticed recently – a glimmer of light, a kind word, a fleeting feeling. Let this act remind you of the strength in staying soft and the beauty your sensitivity brings to the world.

DAY 341: CURATE YOUR LIFE LIKE ART

Think of your life as your most personal masterpiece – a room where every colour, every picture and every piece of furniture reflects you. Imagine this life like your bedroom: you paint the walls, you choose the decor. You wouldn't let someone barge in and hang their own pictures, right? This one life is yours to create, to curate, to make into something undeniably *you*. It's your special project, your ongoing work of art. If there are people or things that no longer serve you, it's time to curate them out. You are the artist here, with the freedom to choose what stays and what goes. Craft a life that feels like home, a space that inspires you and reflects your unique vision. The art of life is in this curation – choosing only what truly belongs.

CHALLENGE

Take 15 minutes to reflect on one area of your life – your physical space, your schedule or your relationships. Identify one thing that no longer serves you or aligns with your vision. Decide how you can 'curate it out' and replace it with something that feels more authentic and inspiring. Take one actionable step today towards creating your masterpiece.

DAY 342: MOVE FASTER THAN YOUR FEAR

Being proactive isn't just about doing – it's about moving quicker than your fears and doubts. Do the work faster than you can talk yourself out of it. Pick up this book before you decide you're too tired to push today. Building new habits and breaking old cycles takes grit, especially in that breakthrough phase – the stage where the butterfly fights free from the chrysalis, that painful, pivotal moment. If you can make it through that moment with quick, proactive choices, you'll emerge transformed. Push through this period with courage, moving faster than hesitation, and you'll come out on the other side unrecognizable, as the truest version of yourself.

CHALLENGE

Identify one task or creative idea you've been hesitating on. Set a timer for 15 minutes and start immediately – before fear or doubt can take over. Focus on action, not perfection, and reflect afterwards on how moving quickly changed your momentum and mindset.

DAY 343: WE CAN ALL EAT

Yes, you – give people a chance. If you want others to take a chance on you, start by extending that same curiosity to those around you. The creative world is buzzing with talent, with people eager to prove themselves, to be seen, to be given an opportunity. If you have the chance to extend a hand, to open a door, *do it*. To *arm your artists* means to reach out, to offer what you have, to create space for others to thrive. There is enough room for all of us to succeed, to create and to share in the joy of making. This isn't a competition – it's a community. When you support other creatives, you build a culture of abundance, where generosity and growth coexist. So, let's arm each other with chances, with collaboration and with the belief that we are stronger together. There is space here for all of us to eat, create and elevate each other.

CHALLENGE

Reach out to a fellow creative today – someone you admire, someone starting out or someone who could use encouragement. Offer a genuine compliment, a piece of advice or an opportunity to collaborate. Take one action to contribute to the culture of abundance, showing that there's room for everyone to succeed.

DAY 344: MINDFUL

Let's be mindful today. Make some choices – real ones. If you want to spend the day on your phone, scrolling and zoning out, do it with intention, with 100% of your focus. But if you want to be awake, alive, making moves towards what you love, then make that choice with everything you've got. Being mindful means knowing where your time goes and who it goes to. It's the mindlessness that drains your energy, that pulls you away from your art, little by little. If you succumb to the doom scroll, to people-pleasing and to every boundary you refuse to make – what's left for your craft? Nothing. Today, reclaim your time and attention. Make choices that keep you connected to what matters. Your art, your goals and the life you're building deserve every bit of that mindful energy.

CHALLENGE

Track how you spend your time today. Write down each activity in a journal or note, even the small ones. At the end of the day, reflect on how much of your time was spent mindfully and aligned with your goals versus mindlessly. Identify one change you can make tomorrow to reclaim your focus and energy for what matters most.

DAY 345: BREAK THE CYCLE

How many days this year have died to your own hesitation? You're caught in the same cycle, day in and day out. It's day 345 . . . are we still doing this halfway? Take a look at yourself right now. Are you faking that this means something, skimming along, promising you'll change 'soon'? Right now, you might feel fired up. But what happens in 2 hours when a call from that energy vampire leaves you drained, every last drop sucked dry? You don't have to keep listening just because you're used to it. You don't have to stay stuck, stay quiet, stay in cycles that never lead anywhere. Today, make the choice to wake up. Decide that this ends here. Break the cycle and start living fully, not halfway. The future you're waiting for is waiting for *you* to make a real move.

CHALLENGE

Identify one cycle in your life that keeps holding you back – whether it's hesitation, distraction or a draining relationship. Take one concrete action today to disrupt that pattern. Say no, set a boundary, start the task you've been avoiding – whatever it takes to signal to yourself that the cycle ends now. Write down how it feels to take this step towards freedom.

DAY 346: NOTHING IS CEMENT

Did you know you can change anything about your life? Right now, if you wanted, you could move somewhere new, meet different people, find a new favourite café and completely rewrite your routine. Nothing in this life is set in stone. If you feel stuck, ask yourself – what's your art like? Is it an escape, a way to travel to new places, or is it as stuck as you feel? Is that why you haven't made anything in a while? Stagnation feels like salt poured on a slug, paralyzing, a slow decline from the spark that once lit you up. But remember – this feeling of 'just the way things are' is an illusion. You are not stuck. Your soul is craving a breakthrough, aching for growth and change. So, shake things up. Let yourself expand, stretch beyond what you know, and watch how your art comes alive when you finally let go of everything that's been holding you back.

CHALLENGE

Identify one aspect of your routine or creative process that feels stagnant. Change it up today – take a new route, try a different medium or shift your workspace. Do one thing that feels unfamiliar or out of your comfort zone, and reflect on how this change sparks new energy or ideas in your art.

DAY 347: BUILDING YOUR BELIEFS

Right now, you're building your beliefs, laying down the foundation of who you're going to be. Think of the drama teacher in her clogs and poncho – the only clothing free enough to match her spirit. She didn't just arrive there; choices were made, one at a time, until her style became a natural fit, echoing her habits and passions. Maybe you're in that phase too. Testing, trying on ideas, figuring out what will stick. And it's okay if your sense of identity is bigger than any single choice or style right now. This is your becoming, your evolution into something real and uniquely yours. So, keep going. Let every choice, every experiment, add to the version of you that's unfolding. Because the path you're on is leading you somewhere special.

CHALLENGE

Choose one small, intentional action today that aligns with the version of yourself you're becoming. Whether it's wearing something bold, starting a habit or diving into a passion project, let this choice reflect your evolving identity. At the end of the day, reflect on how it felt to step into this version of you.

DAY 348: FACE YOURSELF

It's time to face yourself. Face the parts of you that scare you, the shadows that linger just out of sight. If you feel bitterness creeping in, ask yourself: did it start with jealousy, with anger? Sometimes, one deeply rooted emotion evolves, changing shape until it becomes unrecognizable. Check yourself before you wreck yourself – there's wisdom in that. Don't let these feelings live inside you too long. Before you know it, forgiveness feels out of reach, and the weight of things you've held onto will cloud not just your heart but also your art. Clear out the spaces you hold onto, release what doesn't serve you and let yourself create from a place that's free and open. This is how you make room for the truth that's waiting to flow through you.

CHALLENGE

Take 15 minutes to sit with your emotions today. Identify one feeling you've been avoiding or suppressing – jealousy, anger, regret – and write about its roots. Where did it come from? How has it evolved? Then, write a release statement, letting go of that emotion. Use this exercise to clear space for your creativity to flow freely.

DAY 349: FEEL THE AIR

What does the air feel like today? What do you smell, what do you hear? Check in with your space – is it safe, inviting? Whatever weight or tension you feel around you, take a deep breath. The atmosphere is thick but remember, you hold the power. You carry the golden energy that can shift any room, any creative space. Right now, just by breathing, you're already changing the energy around you for the better. So go forth with that intention. Create today knowing it's already amazing simply because you showed up. If you're worried that inspiration won't come, trust that it will. You being here is enough. Let that truth settle in and create from there.

CHALLENGE

Pause and take three deep, intentional breaths. Pay attention to the sensations around you – the air, the sounds, the smells. Then, create something today inspired by your immediate environment, whether it's a sketch, a journal entry or a quick photo. Let the act of being present guide your creativity.

DAY 350: IT'S HEAVY

As creatives, we're constantly called to see the unseen, hear the unheard and bring the non-existent into existence. If you're tired today, thank God – so are we. It's okay to feel this weight because this is more than just a dream; it's something we were born with, an innate pull to transform the intangible into something real. Seeing the world this way is a gift, but it's also exhausting. The endless inspiration, the perpetual hunt for beauty, depth and truth – it takes a toll. So, give yourself a moment. Breathe. Honour the amazing capacity you have but remember that rest is part of the journey too.

CHALLENGE

Take 30 minutes today to rest intentionally. Step away from your creative project, find a quiet spot and let yourself recharge without guilt. Reflect on one way that rest fuels your creativity and write it down as a reminder to honour your need for balance.

DAY 351: SAVOUR THE MOMENT

Whatever stage of the process you're in – savour it, especially when everything is clicking. When you're in love with what you're making; when you find that part of yourself willing to stay up late to chase a thread of inspiration; when the risks you took are finally paying off, this is the magic of creativity. It's rich, layered and full of unexpected delights. These moments are fleeting but powerful. Hold onto them, let them fill you up and savour every bit.

CHALLENGE

Pause during your creative process today and take 5 minutes to reflect on what you love about this moment. Write it down or capture it in a photo or voice note. Let this act of savouring become a memory you can return to when the process feels tough.

DAY 352: POSSIBILITIES

The best art doesn't come from repeating yesterday's moves but from stretching into tomorrow's possibilities. As creators, we often feel the pull to stay safe, to reach for the tried and true. But staying there? It means only grasping what's already been found. The unfamiliar, the wild unknown – that's where real risk/reward lives. It's the edge of comfort, the far side of familiar, where ideas collide in unexpected ways. So today, lean into the space beyond what you've always done. That's where the best discoveries wait.

CHALLENGE

Try something completely new in your creative process today – whether it's a technique, a tool or a bold idea you've never explored. Step beyond what feels comfortable and reflect afterwards on how this stretch sparked new possibilities for your work.

DAY 353: BUILD, DON'T PERFORM

You can fake it – for a little while. But in the end, the truth catches up. Are you here to put on a show or to make something real? Putting in the hours isn't glamorous and it doesn't come with applause. But imagine the confidence that builds when you know your work isn't just a string of magic tricks, but a solid foundation you've built yourself. Skip the shortcuts today. Step into the effort, the grit, the hours, and build something that's yours. Not for anyone else, not for appearances – but because you're done performing and ready to stand on what you've actually created. That's all.

CHALLENGE

Dedicate an hour today to a part of your creative process that feels unglamorous or tedious but essential. Focus on the foundation – whether it's practising a skill, refining details or organizing ideas. Embrace the effort as a step towards building something real and lasting.

DAY 354: TAKE CARE OF YOURSELF

How's your mind today? Have you paused to check in with yourself on this creative journey? Becoming the best version of yourself means caring for your mind, too. Some days will be clear and inspired, others messy and complicated – but every day, your mental wellness is essential to the art you're creating. Creating requires vulnerability, and with every piece you put out, you're opening yourself up. It's powerful, but it's also essential to take time to properly 'close up shop' at the end of the day. Ensuring your mind doesn't spiral or get lost in the openness of creation is a form of self-care, one that strengthens you as an artist. Are you giving yourself time to decompress, to let your imagination breathe? Step back, reconnect with the reasons you create and allow yourself to be grounded in the present. Take care of your mind so it can go the distance and fuel your art.

CHALLENGE

Set aside 20 minutes today for a mental reset. Whether it's journalling, meditating, taking a walk or simply sitting in silence, use this time to decompress and reconnect with yourself. Reflect on how this pause impacts your clarity and creative energy and make it a regular part of your routine.

DAY 355: BE PREPARED

This is the moment to be ready. They say preparation met with opportunity is what makes luck, and if you're not ready, it's time to get there and stay there. You're far enough along this path to know that surprises come at every turn. Don't let yourself be caught off guard. Arrive with options, bring your ideas and step up ready to play ball. Success doesn't come from starting at the buzzer – it's the hours, the notes, the sweat you put in long before anyone is watching. Your training off the clock, the late nights spent perfecting your craft – that's what counts. Stay ready, so when the moment comes, you can step into it fully prepared to own it.

CHALLENGE

Choose one aspect of your craft that you want to be ready for when opportunity strikes. Spend 30 minutes today practising, refining or preparing for that moment – whether it's rehearsing a pitch, perfecting a skill or organizing your ideas. Let this preparation build your confidence and keep you ready for whatever comes next.

DAY 356: BELIEVE IT'S YOURS

Today is the day you believe it's yours. It's not just about what you want; it's about believing you're worthy of it. Somewhere along the way, some experience – some doubt or shame – took a shot at your confidence. Now, maybe you can't even picture a life where you deserve it. Or maybe you do believe in yourself without a shadow of a doubt and know this is your path. Either way, believing it's yours can be a challenge as a creative. The road to success is rarely a straight line, but trust in the quiet, steady pulse that pulls you towards it. This is your life, your vision. If you can learn to believe in it, no matter the setbacks, you're already halfway there.

CHALLENGE

Write down one goal or dream you've been hesitant to fully claim as yours. Then, write a declaration: 'This is mine, and I am worthy of it.' Say it out loud to yourself and take one small action today that aligns with owning this belief. Let this be the first step towards making it a reality.

DAY 357: GIVE BACK WHAT YOU FOUND

As you reach the end of this journey, consider how your work can lift other creatives up. Creativity is a gift – a gift that becomes far sweeter when shared. How can you offer it back? Be the mentor, the friend or the guide you once needed. Remember the moments when someone reached out a hand, gave you advice or just believed in you. Be that for someone else. We all need that person in our lives who sees our potential before we can. You only get one life and it's so much more powerful when you share it, building something beautiful that could only exist because of you. Embrace that role – create not just for yourself but for a world that thrives on the contributions of each of us. Lift others as you continue to rise and you'll see how your gift keeps on giving.

CHALLENGE

Think of one person who could benefit from your unique gift, encouragement or perspective today. Reach out to them with a thoughtful word, gesture or action and let your creativity be the connection they need.

DAY 358: LETTING GO IS POWER

The problems that once took up every ounce of your mental space – those worries, the hurt, the doubts – they don't even belong to you anymore. They don't fit who you are now. You've evolved, gained the tools and resilience that the old you didn't have. The artist who once felt stifled or hurt is now ready to fly, strengthened by growth and perspective. Letting go isn't just moving on; it's claiming the power you've earned by growing through the struggle. The past can rest, and you can rise. Read that back one more time. The past can rest, and you can rise.

CHALLENGE

Identify one lingering worry, doubt or hurt that no longer fits who you've become. Write it down on a piece of paper, then destroy it – tear it up, burn it (safely) or throw it away. Use this act as a symbolic release, making space for the strength and growth you've earned.

DAY 359: WHAT IS MEANT FOR YOU IS COMING

There's a unique thrill in the life of an artist, isn't there? Some of the greatest things to ever shape your journey will appear when you least expect it – dropped right into your lap, like a gift from the universe. Projects you've fought tirelessly for will pave the way, and then, out of nowhere, something will arrive that changes everything. It fills you with a purpose so deep, a pride so real, you'll wonder how you ever lived without it. That's the beauty of this path. Every day holds a spark, a possibility, a hint of magic. For an artist, the journey is a mix of determination and unexpected grace. Stay open, stay ready – your best moments are waiting, just around the corner.

CHALLENGE

Take a moment today to reflect on the unexpected gifts that have shaped your creative journey so far. Write down one thing you're working towards and remind yourself: what is meant for you is on its way. Then, take one step – big or small – to stay open and prepared for the opportunities that lie ahead.

DAY 360: ART WILL SAVE US

Why is it that our darkest moments ignite such a hunger to create, a craving to pour ourselves into something tangible? Maybe it's because in those moments, art becomes a lifeline. When life feels overwhelming or pain seems too heavy to carry alone, the need to make meaning out of it grows urgent. There's something powerful in taking what hurts, what haunts, and reshaping it into something beautiful, something that speaks. Art allows us to bring light to the shadows, to take control of emotions that feel larger than life. Creating becomes a way to transcend, to transform darkness into insight, pain into purpose. It's in these moments of raw honesty that we find not only relief but also a way to connect, to share and to feel understood. This is the gift of art – it lets us turn what's heavy into something that lifts us up.

CHALLENGE

Take a feeling or experience that feels heavy right now and channel it into a creative act. Write a poem, paint a picture, compose a melody – whatever feels natural to you. Let this be an honest expression of what you're carrying and allow the process to transform the weight into something meaningful. Reflect on how this act of creation shifts your perspective.

DAY 361: A LIFE OF MEANING

You'll never regret a single day spent digging within yourself, searching for meaning and making something of it. This life we've chosen – the life of a creator – is rare and beautiful. It's a blessing, a gift, whatever you want to call it. To have the ability to turn ideas into form, to make beauty where there was nothing before, is nothing short of magic. In a world that often overlooks the quiet, vulnerable work of making meaning, we know how special this is. To create is to find a way to transcend the ordinary, to carve out pockets of truth and beauty from within ourselves and offer them to the world. And in doing so, we're reminded every day just how extraordinary this gift really is.

CHALLENGE

Reflect on what creating has brought to your life – whether it's meaning, joy or connection. Write down three specific moments where your creativity made an impact, on yourself or others. Use this reflection as a reminder of why you chose this path and let it fuel your next creative act.

DAY 362: WHY YOU? BECAUSE YOU

No one else could bring it like you can. Your unique *hard-won perspective* – all the experiences, challenges and quiet moments of growth you've been through – has shaped a voice and vision that no one else has. You didn't stumble onto this perspective; you earned it, bit by bit. It's the scars, the triumphs and the quiet realizations that make your view unlike anyone else's. When you wonder, 'Why me?' – the answer will always be 'Because you.' Because no one else has lived your story, seen what you've seen, or felt your particular blend of heartbreak and joy. Your creativity comes from those hard-won layers of you. So, lean in, show up and remember: you're here because only *you* can bring *you* to life.

CHALLENGE

Write a short reflection about one experience or moment that has shaped your perspective as a creator. How does it influence the way you see, feel or make? Use this reflection as inspiration for a creative piece today – something that only you could create because it comes from your unique story.

DAY 363: THE MORE YOU KNOW

The deeper you go, the harder it becomes – not because you're any less capable, but because you *know* more. Each stroke now carries the weight of experience, precision and purpose. The days of winging it fade, and knowledge adds a new kind of weight. Expectation creeps in, whispering that you should know better, create better. This is the paradox of mastery. The more you understand, the greater the responsibility to do justice to that understanding. So, when creating feels heavier, recognize it as a sign of growth. You're not losing your edge; you're gaining depth, and that's where real artistry takes root. Keep going – embrace the difficulty, for it's a testament to how far you've come.

CHALLENGE

Reflect on one area of your craft where you've gained significant knowledge or skill over time. Identify a challenge you've been avoiding because it feels 'heavier' now with your expertise. Tackle it head-on today, using your growth as a tool to push through and create something meaningful. Celebrate the depth you've earned.

DAY 364: PARTICIPATING VS. CONTRIBUTING

Today's culture pushes creators to contribute before they've even found their voice. Often, we feel pressure to have something bold to say from day one. But perhaps it's less about arriving with a statement and more about beginning with curiosity, showing up to create before we define what we want to contribute. When you're new to creating – or even returning after a break – it's natural to want to make an impact. But sometimes, growth comes from simply participating, from trying, experimenting and letting yourself be surprised. Real discovery happens when you give yourself room to make a mess, to get it wrong and to see what resonates within you. Your voice finds you, not the other way around. Authentic work emerges once you've spent time exploring without pressure. Start by showing up, letting go of the need to have it all figured out, and trust that your voice will take shape when you give it the space to breathe.

CHALLENGE

Dedicate today to participating without pressure. Choose a creative activity – sketching, writing, playing music or anything that feels natural – and approach it with curiosity, not perfection. Let yourself explore without the need to produce something 'bold' or 'finished'. Reflect afterwards on what surprised or resonated with you in the process.

DAY 365: THANK YOU

Thank yourself for being here – for every moment you showed up, for every step forward, for every idea you brought to life. Thank yourself for choosing to create, even on the days it felt impossible. For trusting your vision, for pushing through doubt, for honouring your creativity in ways big and small. This year has been a testament to your dedication, a body of work shaped by your hands, fuelled by your passion. That is worth celebrating.

Let this be a reminder: you are capable of so much more than you know. Keep going. Keep honouring your creativity. Keep making, exploring and daring to bring your ideas to life. The world is better because you choose to create. And if we can fill 365 pages with inspiration, we promise you can do anything you set your mind to. Thank you for showing up. Thank you for believing in yourself. This is just the beginning.

Keep creating and repeating.

CHALLENGE

Share this book with someone who inspires you or someone who could use a spark. Pass it on.

ACKNOWLEDGEMENTS

To our families – thank you for your unwavering support, love and belief in us through every step of this process. To our parents and sisters, your encouragement carried us through the late nights, creative blocks and moments of doubt. We're endlessly grateful.

To our dog, Happy Boy – you are pure love on four legs. Thank you for being our constant, our emotional support and our reminder to take breaks and go outside.

And finally, this book is dedicated to our son, Sunny Jude Evans. You are our light. The release of this book and your due date being the same day is no coincidence – it's divine timing. No matter the ups and downs we've faced, you and this book have always been our shimmering bright light at the end of the tunnel. We are writing the things we wish existed in this world, for you. So that as you grow and navigate your own creative life, you feel seen. We write for you. We breathe for you. We live for you. However we can support you in this lifetime, whether as a creative or whatever else you choose to be, we will be here for you. Always.

Love,
Mom and Dad

NOTES